About the Author

JACQUELYN B. FLETCHER is a freelance writer, stepdaughter, and stepmother of three young children. She writes often about stepfamilies in publications including *Daughters* online magazine, and has contributed to numerous other publications. A marketing and publishing professional, she also teaches writing classes at the Loft Literary Center in Minneapolis, Minnesota, where she lives. Visit www.becomingastepmom.com.

A CAREER GIRL'S GUIDE

to Becoming a

STEPMOM

A CAREER GIRL'S GUIDE

to Becoming a

STEPMOM

**EXPERT ADVICE FROM OTHER STEPMOMS ON HOW TO
JUGGLE YOUR JOB, YOUR MARRIAGE,
AND YOUR NEW STEPKIDS**

JACQUELYN B. FLETCHER
FOREWORD BY FRANCESCA ADLER-BAEDER, PH.D.

HARPER

NEW YORK • LONDON • TORONTO • SYDNEY

HARPER

HarperCollins books may be purchased for educational, business, or sales promotional use. For information please write: Special Markets Department, HarperCollins Publishers, 10 East 53rd Street, New York, NY 10022.

FIRST EDITION

Designed by Jan Pisciotta

Library of Congress Cataloging-in-Publication Data

Fletcher, Jacquelyn B.
    A career girl's guide to becoming a stepmom : expert advice from other stepmoms on how to juggle your job, your marriage, and your new stepkids / by Jacquelyn B. Fletcher ; foreword by Francesca Adler-Baeder.
        p. cm.
    ISBN: 978-0-06-084683-1
    ISBN-10:   0-06-084683-6
        1. Stepmothers. 2. Women in the professions. I. Title.

HQ759.92.F54 2007
306.874'7—dc22

                                                                    2006052598

13 14 15 16   ID/RRD   10 9 8 7 6 5 4

For my three wonderful stepchildren and Arne.
I love you all.

To my parents and stepparents who didn't have the
benefit of stepfamily research to guide them.
And to the many passionate stepfamily researchers
and professionals who really are making it easier for
stepfamilies to succeed.

Contents

Foreword

Y ou are a single career woman who is about to marry a man with children from a previous relationship. My social science colleagues have studied you; I have taught about you in my college Marriage and Family courses. You're a part of a growing trend spanning several decades.

Since the women's movement, when opportunities opened up for women, and men were no longer our primary route to economic stability, increasing numbers of college- and post-graduate-educated women emerged. We know that having a higher level of education and income is related to a later-than-average first marriage (the average for all women is currently age twenty-three). We also know that a "marriage gradient" persists in our culture. That is, men are typically older than the women they marry. So, if a woman waits to marry until her late twenties, thirties, or forties, the likelihood of falling in love with and marrying a man who has been previously married increases with every passing year. And more than likely that man has children, and she will become a stepmom.

In the last two decades, information has been generated

on stepfamily experiences and offered through clinical training, community education programs, Websites, and online forums, and books for self-study. In my professional life as a family scientist and stepfamily researcher, and in my personal life as a stepfamily member, I have had the opportunity to review many and varied forms of resources. Jacquelyn Fletcher's book, *A Career Girl's Guide to Becoming a Stepmom*, is utterly unique—and necessary.

Jacque has recognized that her experience as a "career girl" turned stepmom is not rare. She knows you are there—this sorority of women. She also has recognized that despite the age of "information overload" that we live in, ironically, information to empower you is virtually nonexistent. And certainly, the approach she takes is absolutely unprecedented. She combines real women's experiences, research information, and a businesswoman's framework in order to provide a strategy-focused approach to building a loving, nurturing marriage and stepfamily.

There is so much I love about this book! Part of what I love is what is *not* in this book. What you will not find are the lengthy rantings of frustrated women who have found themselves in challenging situations and who provide warnings and roadmaps with each potential problem clearly highlighted. When I think back over the number of books I've read, the presentations I've seen, and the discussions I've heard about stepfamily experiences the majority fall into this category. But Jacque brings a healthy and fresh new approach.

Although certainly, we as human beings can feel a need to vent and to seek acknowledgment and identification with our challenges, knowledgeable professionals in the field of human development and family relationships will always ask the next question: So what helps? What strategies can you employ as an individual to move this experience in a positive direction? I believe all individuals want to take this next step, too; they often just don't realize it. It can be quite comforting to commiserate with others. In fact, I've been witness to long-running "support" groups (and I use quotes for a reason) that fuel each other's negative feelings toward the situations and people they are sharing information about—as a show of "support." If this is the end of the support experience, what is ultimately the benefit to the person? How have things changed? More important, how has this person gained knowledge of how to effect change?

Here is the key to this book—and the reason every word resonated with me. I advocate in my professional and personal life an empowerment approach, and clearly Jacque and I belong to the same sisterhood. An empowerment approach to life means that you inform yourself, you open your eyes, you make yourself aware of what may lie ahead—but then, you take action. You utilize a vision of where you want to be and you become *intentional* about how you get there. In teaching about relationships and marriages, people often refer to the importance of "working at" and "being committed to" a relationship. I don't like these terms. "Working at" seems to imply a sort of unemotional drudgery. And *commitment* is too abstract a word for me. I think that being *intentional* evokes a picture of positive, energetic action—implementing strategies, concrete things to do.

Jacque is masterful at providing clear strategies for things to do and how to talk to yourself (an extremely important, yet often overlooked dimension of relational skills). I have never reviewed a book for stepfamilies that gives the reader such clear instructions and pictures. I have a confession, too. Though I have studied and worked with stepfamilies for almost two decades, and am living in a stepfamily, even I was marking in the margins "try this" and "recommend this!"

I love her use of business development and work environment models as a framework for prescribing strategies for building your stepfamily relationships. It makes so much sense to be as intentional about our success in our families as we are about our success at work. No matter what your career path is or has been, I know that you will feel empowered as you read her suggestions. You will know you can apply the suggestions, because you will realize that you have used or are currently using these strategies in other contexts.

I love the glimpses of real women's lives that are the heart and soul of this book. You will feel the entire time that you are in a gathering of friends. The emotions and the stories span the spectrum of the human experience. You will be touched and inspired and will laugh out loud again and again. Always, there is a teaching point. One of Jacque's skills is to extract from each story, from each conversation, what it is that we can learn—and what it is that you can do and how that can inform your thinking. She is a loving and caring guide.

I love that throughout the book, explicitly and implicitly, there is a focus on and strategies to develop empathy— empathy for each member of your family. In child development research, we have observed that empathy for others (i.e., consciously taking on another's perspective) is a learned skill. Unfortunately, this does not appear to be an innate trait for human beings. It might be the only thing Freud was right about—we are quite egocentric. And egocentricity is a barrier to healthy human relationships. Empathy begets empathy, and relationships—and the individuals in them—are nurtured in the process.

I love the weaving together of expert information. As a family scientist, I am appreciative of Jacque's many references to "the research of stepfamilies." We have spent many years talking with stepfamily members through formal research projects and have uncovered lots of interesting information on patterns of interactions that work and those that don't. Jacque has done her homework. Although any individual's experiences are always valid, to rely solely on one's own experiences to teach from typically provides incomplete information. In the area of stepfamily resources, I can say that the majority of "educational" books fall in this category. Instead, Jacque brings research-validated information to life through her own stories and the stories of the wonderful women you will read about. In doing so, she also fills in the gaps on yet to be discovered research information. What she taps so well are the identity issues that single, child-free career women turned stepmoms wrestle with. We have not yet begun to tap this through formal research. Her and her group of experts' insights are powerful, touching, and enlightening.

I love (have I said I love this book?) that this book is about creating a healthy marriage. This is a book to share with your husband. There is information in here to promote empathy be-tween you. There is information in here to build your skills as a couple. The desire to grow a long-lasting, fulfilling marriage is central throughout the stories and Jacque's self-reflections. In reading this book, I never once lost sight of this. The children your husband brings into the marriage are an important focus and much of your energy and time will be devoted to navigating these relationships. This happens while you are simultaneously building strengths in your marriage. Your journey includes this interplay of relationships; one cannot be disentangled from the other. Accept it, arm yourself with the knowledge and strate-gies thoughtfully shared here, and know that you are experi-encing the ultimate modern love story.

Francesca Adler-Baeder, Ph.D.

Department of Human Development and Family Studies,
    Auburn University, Alabama

Director, Center for Children, Youth, and Family

Executive Director, The National Stepfamily Resource Center

A CAREER GIRL'S GUIDE

to Becoming a

STEPMOM

Thirty-Something Single Successful Girl Seeks Mature Male for Dating, Maybe More

I didn't meet my husband until seven months after my thirtieth birthday. The truth is that despite my love of romantic movies and love stories, I wasn't looking for Mr. Right. I spent most of my twenties working hard to create a career. Sure, I dated, but all the wrong guys. There was the sexy man from Argentina, the sweet mountain climber from Montana, the pompous would-be writer from Minneapolis, the tattooed rocker from Chicago, etc., etc.

I wasn't worried about finding a husband; I was too busy having a blast. And unlike what women of earlier generations experienced, no one pressured me. None of my girlfriends from college or my peers at work were married with children. Much like the 30- and 40-something heroines in the piles of chick-lit books in Barnes and Noble and shows such as *Sex in the City*, I was focused on completing my education, building my own business, and hanging with my friends.

Instead of giving birth to a baby (or two, or four) in my first decade as an adult, I created a beautiful single existence with a fabulous apartment, yoga classes, and trips around the world to keep me busy. Instead of hauling a toddler to playdates with other mothers, I networked with clients. I figured I would get married *someday* in a land far, far away and have children in my mid- to late thirties, maybe even in my early forties.

My family had long ago stopped giving me grief about finding a nice young man and instead asked me questions about my business and friends. They occasionally teased me about my predilection for dating artists, and voiced the hope that I'd someday settle down with a nice khaki-pants man. But other than that, they didn't bug me about it.

Yet in the quiet moments when I was home alone thinking about my visions for the future, I did see myself at 85 years old with a husband, children, and grandchildren surrounding me.

A few months before I met my husband, I decided I was tired of hanging out with the wrong men. I didn't want to "ooh" and "ahh" and pretend I was interested in any more boys who were just not right for me. I was done. So I decided to wait for what I wanted. I decided to say "No," and sometimes, "No way!" until he arrived. And I vowed that when he showed up, I would be open to love in whatever form it decided to take.

Then I met Arne, a khaki-pants man with an artist's soul.
I went to a party with my brother that his M.B.A. classmates
threw at a Minneapolis hot spot. A few moments after I'd
walked in, ordered and received a dirty martini, a woman I'd
met once before came running up to me. "These guys over here
want to meet you," she enthused. I figured they were friends
of my brother and agreed to accompany her across the room
to their table. "Make sure you talk to the one with the dimples
and the amazing smile," she whispered as we approached.

The hot guy with the smile and I ended up talking all night.
As it turned out, Arne wasn't a friend of my brother's, but had
showed up with his cousin. He was four years older than me,
which was refreshing after all the completely unsuitable boys
barely out of college and the nice but twice-my-age gentle-
men I'd dated. He had presence and wisdom, gentleness and
quiet strength. Instantly, I was intrigued.

Like most of these freaky six-degrees-of-separation stories
go, we knew some of the same people. I was the editor of a
magazine at the time, and he had it on his desk because the
company he worked for advertised in it. He'd seen my picture
and read my Letter from the Editor column. He remembered
thinking I was cute. We laughed and blushed. He ignored his
cousin and I ignored my brother and friends as we got ac-
quainted.

And then he dropped the bombshell. He was divorced.
Okay, I thought. My parents were divorced, and so was my
brother. I was cool with that. Then he told me about his three
kids. I could feel apprehension shoot through my body. "Oh,
really?" He pulled out his wallet and showed me a holiday

portrait of three young children. The blond cherubs dressed in matching finery smiled at the camera. "Wow, they're cute," was all I could think to say. My mouth was suddenly bone-dry. I had a moment of vertigo as I caught a glimpse of a world completely different from the life I was living as a single girl in the city.

"You're not going to walk away?" he asked after he put the photo back in his wallet.

"No."

There was something in his eyes. And I had promised myself I would be open to love no matter what. He asked for my number and called me the next morning at 10 A.M. We set our first date for a week later. And that was it.

I fell in love, and fell hard, despite the divorce, the ex, and the kids. A year and half later, we married. And at the moment I became a wife, I became the stepmother of three children, like both my mother and my own stepmother.

My experience with stepfamilies began when I was 11, after my parents divorced and I acquired a new stepmom and stepdad. I have spent a lifetime making family out of step-, half, and blood relatives.

Back then my parents and stepparents didn't have the benefit of years of family science research to help them create successful stepfamilies. They made practically every common mistake I describe in this book. From age 5, I was placed in a loyalty conflict trying to protect each side from the other. I remember feeling terrified in those early years of what was occurring in my home. And as happens to so many children of divorce,

I had to grow up fast because I felt I had to parent my parents. As a result, I felt rejected, fearful, sad, and responsible.

Then when I hit my teens, I rebelled. The anger in me at my parents and stepparents grew to a fever pitch, and in what I later found out was a textbook case, I acted out my rage by testing every boundary I could. And I hated them all. They had made my life hell by ripping away my safe home, and I wanted them all to pay for what they'd done to me.

That could have been the end of the story. I hung out with the wrong crowd. I smoked. I drank. I was 100 pounds overweight. The hatred was killing me because I'd turned it inward. Thankfully, in my early twenties I finally understood I had to do something to turn my life around. I looked at myself and imagined what would happen to me if I kept living the lifestyle I'd chosen. I didn't want to be the kid who could never get over her parents' divorce. I didn't want my parents' actions to have that much control over me. So I practiced acceptance. I worked to find peace about my past. I quit smoking. I started to exercise and eat healthy and lost the 100 pounds. Over time I came to see all the things my parents had done to keep us together as a family, on both sides. Now, decades later, I have two loving and supportive stepfamilies and a family of my own. I've learned things that work and things that don't when building a stepfamily. I've tried the strategies. I've failed. I've been angry and hopeless and frustrated. But I've also seen what works.

From the stepmothers, adult stepchildren, and stepfamily professionals I interviewed for this book, I heard the same stories, almost word for word, over and over again. It was eerie how often I heard my own life story from complete strangers, some living thousands of miles from me.

I kept thinking, "If stepfamilies continue to fail at such alarming rates, and the stories are all about the same things, what isn't working? And how can we fix it so our families do work?"

According to the U.S. Census, approximately 1,300 new stepfamilies are formed every single day, and there are more than 15 million stepmothers in the United States. Estimates suggest stepfamilies currently outnumber nuclear families, and no one—not even people in stepfamilies—knows that. There is a surprising shortage of resources for new stepmothers—those with children of their own and those who have never married before. Yet within the last two decades more research has been done about stepfamilies than ever before. There is help out there, but stepfamilies are not accessing the resources available.

Most of the families I talked to approached their new roles by just winging it until they hit a problem. And only then did they seek help. I found that many new or soon-to-be stepmothers didn't know how or where to find information. They were so overwhelmed by the work of adjusting to a new life that all they could do was try to survive, instead of feel the bliss of opening to new relationships and experiences.

There is a tectonic shift occurring in today's American families that is affecting more people every day. With divorce rates in our country hovering at 50 percent for first marriages and between 60 and 70 percent for second marriages that include children, there are legions of human beings who are left adrift in a world of pain and disillusionment.

❖ ❖ ❖

This is a book about love. It's about hope. It's about building a family that is strong and solid, in which each individual member makes the whole stronger. This book is not about instant gratification or a quick fix. *A Career Girl's Guide to Becoming a Stepmom* is for single career women, with no kids of their own, who are dating, engaged to, or married to a man with children from a previous marriage. Estimates suggest that 75 percent of divorced men remarry, 40 percent of all marriages include one partner who has been married before, and 65 percent of remarriages include children from a previous relationship. The numbers are staggering, and they don't even take into account the rising number of couples with children from previous partners who choose to cohabitate and not marry or the number of women in partnerships with other women who have kids.

When I became the stepmother of three children under 10 years old, I frantically searched for help. I found a handful of books that scared the hell out of me about the realities of stepmotherhood. But I felt that none of the resources spoke to the unique problems I was having as a successful, professional woman who was reduced to helplessness and hopelessness at home. I couldn't find a single book dedicated to the growing number of career women who have waited to marry until later in life and suddenly must run a household that includes children.

In the 1980s, Patricia Papernow, a psychologist, stepmother, and author of the award-winning book for therapists, *Becoming a Stepfamily: Patterns of Development in Remarried*

Families, identified seven cycles stepfamilies pass through as they build a life together. Starting with a fantasy and illusion period, they run through immersion, awareness, mobilization, and action as everyone tries to find their place in this new entity, and finally, in some cases after twelve years or more, they end at resolution—otherwise known as stability and commitment. According to Papernow, the rare families who go through the stepfamily cycles quickest can successfully establish their new household within four years—but a majority of stepfamilies don't even make it to the fourth year. And of those stepmothers who slog through years of hard work, many of them still hold deep resentment in their hearts. Is that really a successful stepfamily?

Something is not working. The current strategies and workbooks, the therapy and support groups, are not working because most families don't even know these resources exist. And to make matters worse, according to Margorie Engel, former president of the Stepfamily Association of America, stepfamilies don't consider themselves a stepfamily until there's a problem. Up to that point, they define themselves as simply a nuclear family. But overlooking the ways in which stepfamilies are different often leads to disaster and heartbreak.

The shiny happy family we're all supposed to emulate is a complete fabrication. The instant love and feelings of connectedness and home are not automatic in a stepfamily, so we feel like failures. And yet, we stepmoms are often not willing to do the work it takes to succeed in building a strong stepfamily. We are often unwilling to feel uncomfortable in the moment as we work for long-term success. We sometimes act like victims and don't take responsibility for our part in creating conflict in the early stages of stepfamily development. And in the chaos of the first years, it can be hard to put yourself in your stepkids' or spouse's shoes.

Stepfamilies are here to stay, and it is crucial that stepmoms learn how to address their challenges in a way that promotes positive growth for everyone involved. In order for stepfamilies to thrive, it is imperative that stepmothers do not feel like strangers or prisoners or outsiders in their own homes. Women must feel like they have a say. However, that doesn't mean steamrolling the stepfamily into doing only what the stepmom thinks is appropriate. It's a balancing act— one that takes a great deal of maturity.

There is an upside. Stepfamily life can be a rip-roaring good time. Since few of the former models of family life are working, we get to create a new kind of dynamic in our homes—one that fits us and sustains us. Think of the power! All it takes is creativity, education, the willingness to look at the big picture and ride out the tough times, and the commitment to be present in each moment and each new experience. Easy, right?

To the single woman who has never been married before and has no children of her own, joining an existing family can be incredibly scary. The learning curve is so steep it can bury many a successful businesswoman. Consider this. In the first year of marriage, a stepmother feels she must learn how to live with another human being (or several), learn how to be married, learn how to be a stepmother, with all its thorny issues, find her place within a family that has already been together for years, figure out how to assert herself, learn how to support and communicate with people who are wounded, and learn to deal with the ex. And that's just the tip of the iceberg.

So what's the big payoff? Why do it? Why are there 15 million stepmothers in America and 1,300 new stepfamilies forming every single day? Why are we marrying these men with their broods and their ex-wives?

Simple. Love and hope.

We are battling statistics that seem to be hugely stacked against us, and yet to define ourselves as an "at-risk" group as a new stepfamily is to cut ourselves off at the knees. It becomes a self-fulfilling prophecy.

I'm not going to lie. This will be one of the most difficult things you will ever do. There are times when you're going to feel the darkness of absolute hopelessness descend upon you. And you're going to cry your eyes out. And there will be times, that, yes, even you, will be reduced to throwing what feels like a 14-year-old's hormone-fueled tantrum. There will be times when you'll say to yourself that the journey to feeling at home in your own home is so distant, so insurmountable, why even bother? Take heart. You have the skills. At the office, there's a learning curve no matter how much education or confidence you have. It took experience on the job for you to learn how to succeed. It's the same at home when you join a stepfamily.

Women have helped raise other women's children for as long as humans have existed. So why is it so difficult today? I believe it's our culture of individuation and separateness, in which "I" has become more important than "we." We don't know how to be in relationships with other people today in a self-affirming way that supports all involved. We don't know how to walk our own paths and be true to ourselves when there are people with needs different from our own constantly pulling on our sleeves.

But it can be done. There is something beyond "and they lived happily ever after." There is a way to create a successful stepfamily. And this book will show you one way to start. Be warned: There is no easy answer. You'll need to see what works for you and your family. The research on stepfamilies has been done. The tools are out there to help us be successful (for example, www.stepfamilies.info). So why not access them? Why not make this challenging process as easy on ourselves as possible and not make the obvious, common mistakes?

It can work. It will take work. Like any nuclear family, you need to keep your eye on the larger vision to help you through the day-to-day challenges. Your stepfamily will test your emotional strength. It will stretch you to the limits. But it will also yield the most beautiful results. And you don't have to wait twenty years to enjoy your marriage or your stepchildren. You can decide to enjoy them every day if you want to.

This book will help you get clear about your reasons for creating a stepfamily and provide a roadmap to a successful one. It will let you in on the secrets that successful stepmothers know. It will point you to the places you can go to for more help. Becoming a stepmother is one of the most challenging things a woman can do, but like everything in life, it all comes down to your attitude: how you decide to *be* in the relationships with your new stepchildren and husband. The wonderful thing is, you get to choose.

As career women, we bring assets to a new stepfamily that can help smooth the transition. Consider your skills on the job and how you can apply them to your stepfamily:

- Organization
- Goal setting
- Negotiation
- Dealing with difficult coworkers
- Delaying gratification for long-term success
- Networking
- Problem solving
- Creative brainstorming
- Team building

In this book, you'll see how you can use the skills you already have to create a stepfamily that best fits you, your spouse, the kids, and everyone who comes with them.

Throughout this book you'll find the Career Girl's Personal Assistant to help guide you through the challenges and opportunities of stepmotherhood. Using the training you've received on the job can help you feel confident while you're learning the ropes at home. Your Personal Assistant will help you lay out a plan to help you achieve your goals, whether you want to have a close friendship with a stepchild or support your husband as he deals with a troubled teen.

In Chapter 1, "Cinderella's Man Didn't Have Any Kids;

Why Does Mine?" I address the complex emotions women who marry men with children often feel. You must grieve the death of your childhood fantasies even while you're in the midst of a love affair with the man of your dreams. The exercises in this chapter help you be realistic about what you're getting into, but also help you remember why you are in this relationship in the first place.

In Chapter 2, "What Is a Stepmother?" you'll explore your role. As most husbands of stepmothers know, your expectations of your role can determine an entire family's happiness. This chapter discusses the expectations stepmothers often bring into a new marriage and helps you identify how yours could be generating conflict. You'll also learn to understand how the assumptions of your partner and new stepchildren can influence the stepfamily dynamic.

Chapter 3, "Face the Music," challenges you to step away from the la-la land of love and romance to face reality, namely, the kids. It offers smart strategies for making everyone feel as comfortable as possible on a first meeting and ways to build long-lasting positive relationships using your career woman's strengths at team building and goal setting. You might be used to running the show at work, but even when you join a new company you must learn the culture before you can be effective. This chapter also includes advice from adults who grew up in stepfamilies. The insight offered from these adults can help you avoid some common pitfalls while building a positive relationship with the kids.

Chapter 4, "From Sassy Single to . . . Wife?" includes a checklist of topics to consider before getting married, or even after you're already married, to ensure that yours isn't one of the 60 to 70 percent of second marriages that end in divorce. This chapter helps you put your relationship with your husband front and center so you can approach your stepfamily as a team.

Yet another challenge any couple must face is learning how to live together. Career women who marry and become stepmothers often feel powerless at home. In Chapter 5, "This Land Is My Land," you'll see how day-to-day life in a stepfamily can be managed in order to set up a smoothly running home.

Money is a crucial issue in stepfamilies. The inequality of a new couple's finances is a hot-button issue that must be resolved for future success. In Chapter 6, "Show Me the Money," you'll see how complicated the financial realities in a stepfamily can be and ways to work with what you've got.

Talk to enough stepmothers and you'll find legal horror stories to make your hair stand on end. With everything from fighting custody battles in the first year of a brand-new marriage to getting sued for more child support, stepmothers are often witness to or accomplices in horrific behavior between exes. Chapter 7, "Rocky Road," discusses legal issues stepmothers must know about, including the divorce agreement, pre- or postnuptial agreements, custody issues, child support and alimony requirements, estate planning, legal guardianship, and adoption.

A woman who joins a start-up company knows that her job will be a grand adventure fraught with risks. It's the same when a woman chooses to join a stepfamily. The fact is, you're an adult. You have a choice. You married (or are about to marry) a man with children. Both you and your husband must recognize the power and responsibility in your choice. Chapter 8, "You're the Boss (of Yourself)," helps you identify your power.

Stepmotherhood can drive you to emotional meltdowns the likes of which you haven't experienced since puberty. It's easy for a stepmother with no experience of the realities of stepfamily life to feel like she's crazy and everything is her fault. In Chapter 9, "Pit of Despair," stepmoms share their hard-earned knowledge of the dark places they can go when they are feeling taken advantage of or rejected. It also provides suggestions on how to get out of the pit by taking action.

In Chapter 10, "All Work and No Play Makes Stepmom Wicked," I explore the balance stepmothers can find between doing what they need to do for themselves and spending time with their new stepfamily members.

Chapter 11, "Community Relations," addresses how new stepmoms are now perceived by their bosses, colleagues, friends, and family. When you join a stepfamily, it's a crucial time to assess what your career goals are for the next five, ten, and fifteen years. You must look honestly at how this dynamic will change your relationships.

You also may be surprised that your family isn't supportive of your new marriage or that your new in-laws won't know how to behave. It's important for you and your spouse to outline the ways you'll deal with extended family members together. This chapter will help you identify your personal boundaries in relationships with your colleagues, extended family members, and well-meaning friends who simply don't understand what stepmotherhood entails.

Women tend to be territorial by nature. If you doubt that, try having another woman in your marriage. For stepmothers, having to deal with a woman who is a constant reminder that her beloved has a past can be a hard pill to swallow. Professional women with no kids typically have had the luxury to say good-bye to past loves—even those they were once married to—without having to deal with them on a nearly daily basis for the rest of their lives. In Chapter 12, "The Other Woman," you'll find ways to handle the ex and issues you can expect to crop up, such as jealousy, boundaries, difficulties in scheduling, conflict between your husband and his ex, and emotional tug-of-wars with the children.

Stepmotherhood is more difficult for women who feel pressure to like and even love their husbands' children. In Chapter 13, "Little Monsters," find out what to do when you don't like your new spouse's kids or when they don't like you.

Stepkids aren't the only people who need attention in a stepfamily. Your new husband is the primary reason you're in the stepfamily way in the first place. In Chapter 14, "He Says," you'll find out that men often feel terrible guilt as they watch their new wife and children battle for their places. Here, fathers speak out and offer advice about the issues they face.

In Chapter 15, "Baby on Board?" you'll read about stepmoms who decide to have children with their new husbands. You'll see how a half-sibling can fuse a stepfamily or blow it apart. This chapter provides a checklist of hot topics to consider before you give birth, and helps you develop the relationships between a new baby and your husband's kid(s). You'll also find information about what to do when you can't have a baby.

Chapter 16, "Let the Sun Shine," helps you identify ways you can turn negative thoughts into positive expectations that will help your stepfamily develop strategies for success.

So what does a woman get out of marrying a man with children? In Chapter 17, "The Payoff," you'll see why women stay in stepfamilies for the long haul, and you'll learn how to focus on the big picture.

Finally, I've put together a list of resources that can help you as you create your stepfamily.

So, are you ready? Let's focus on the real reason we're here together. Why did you marry that man? Why are you considering marrying that man? I'd be willing to bet it's pretty simple. Love and hope. And love and hope are things that can sustain you if you decide to open your heart to everyone in your new stepfamily, not just your husband. Those children are there to teach you something. Why not let them?

Cinderella's Man Didn't Have Any Kids; Why Does Mine?

The Fall of the Fantasy

CAREER GIRL'S PERSONAL ASSISTANT

To begin building your stepfamily, use the Career Girl's Personal Assistant to identify how you'll approach stepfamily life. Brainstorm. Discuss. Plan. Implement.

1. Assess your position. Does it match the job description?
2. Gage commitment level. Are you willing to work overtime to discover hidden expectations you have about what you thought your marriage would be like?

3. Identify goals. How many minutes do you want to set aside per day to learn about stepfamily life?
4. Set a meeting time. When will you meet with your husband to discuss your findings from Chapter 1?
5. Encourage teamwork. What fun thing will you do with your husband this week, just the two of you?

So you've lived in that delicious fantasy world for a while: You've met your man and said good-bye to singledom. You're happy. You're in love. So what if he's got kids from a former marriage?

You're a capable woman. You can handle it.

During those first months when you're so in love and still getting to know each other, it's difficult to make a rational decision about the future of your relationship. And even though most stepfamily experts recommend that new couples extend the courtship phase of the relationship until the children have time to adjust, many couples don't, and instead jump naked into the abyss.

Indeed, romantic love is one of the most powerful forces in nature. In a study reported in the July 2005 issue of the *Journal of Neurophysiology*, neuroscientists reproduced images of what happens in our brains when we're in the throes of romantic love. The parts of the brains involved are not connected to sexual impulses, as originally thought, but are in the area that is connected with drives such as hunger, thirst, and drug addiction. Powerful stuff. So it's easy to see why it's hard to educate yourself about the realities of stepfamily life when you're saturated by your feelings for that man. You don't want to hear anything negative, right?

Diane, a journalist and independent radio producer, remembers an exchange that happened when she was engaged to marry her husband, Todd, who had two young boys from a previous marriage. "I was at an event and the woman sitting next to me was a stepmom. When I asked her if she had any advice about becoming a stepmom, she said, 'Don't do it.'" To Diane, who describes meeting Todd at 30 as akin to finding an oasis in the desert, the comment was highly offensive.

But that veteran stepmom's comment reflects how difficult the job of stepmotherhood can be for some women, especially those who are used to running the show at work and living an independent life that is completely dictated by their own wants and needs. The challenge is to maintain and develop your feelings of love for your partner while learning about what you can expect from your new home life—without wanting to jump off the nearest bridge.

Let's get real here, ladies. The fact that your man was married to someone else can be a real bummer. That he, at some point in his life, decided to make a commitment as significant as marriage with another woman might make you feel sick to your stomach. His children from that union are daily reminders that he was intimate with someone else. And that's not fair! None of your ex-boyfriends shows up on your doorstep every single weekend to pick up kids or call several times a week (or day) to negotiate, fight, or coparent.

Before you can begin the work of putting together a satisfying, supportive stepfamily, you need to clear out those negative emotions. You don't want to be a stepmother who, when pressed for details of her stepfamily from a supportive friend two or three decades into the deal, blurts out a stream of resentment she's stored inside the entire time. Sacrificing oneself is not the goal here. Living as present and connected as possible is the goal.

To begin, let's talk about fantasies. Part of the reason stepmotherhood is challenging at the start is because you most likely have a vision of how you want your life to be. When your ideas of how you want to live run headlong into the realities of forming a new stepfamily, the tension can be too much for some women.

Rooting out your fantasies can be a very painful process, but think of it as preventative maintenance. And if you come up with issues you feel you can't handle on your own, by all means find a counselor who is well versed in stepfamily dynamics to help you uncover your fantasies of what your family life should look like and help you move to a place where you can accept and find joy in what is.

Making Space

This book is an interactive experience, just like a stepfamily, and the more you invest of yourself, the more powerful it will be. I recommend purchasing a notebook you can write in about your experiences every day. You'll also need a space for the exercises in this book. I encourage you to do all the exercises as fully as possible and share them with your husband. There are discussion topics for couples at the end of every chapter, which you can each answer separately in writing and then discuss what you've written or simply use as conversation starters.

To begin, interview yourself. Once you have a notebook and a pen, go to your office or a place where you can lock everyone else out. Turn off the phone, PDA, BlackBerry, and e-mail.

Fantasies are powerful. They have deep roots in our psyches that can take years and some painful admissions to uncover. But if we dig up those unspoken beliefs or unrealized dreams, we can examine them so their power over our daily interactions lessens. Answer the questions below to see if any of these common fantasies are influencing you.

Once upon a Time

1. What did you imagine your married life would be like?
2. In what ways is your current situation like what you imagined?
3. In what ways is it different?
4. Is it okay for you to express sadness about the ways in which it is not what you expected? If not, why not? Write down the emotions this brings up for you. Write down all the negative feelings it dredges up even if you'd never admit them to anyone else.
5. When you think of the phrase "It's not fair!" what comes to mind? Throw a tantrum on the page and get it out.

6. What is your definition of family? Write down "My family is ..." ten times and see how many ways you answer that question.
7. What is your vision of yourself at 85 years old? Where are you? Who is with you?
8. What is your family supposed to do for you?
9. Describe what you want your new family to be like.
10. What's your definition of home?

If it helps you get started, here's what it looked like when I began rooting out my fantasies. When I was a little girl, my parents had a long-drawn-out divorce. I became part of two new stepfamilies when both my parents remarried. Even though I saw firsthand the damage people do to one another in the name of love and fear, I still dreamed of meeting my soul mate. And you can be sure he didn't have children from a previous marriage. When I met Arne, I knew he was meant for me. At the same time, I was mad as hell at the world for sending me a man who not only was married before but also had three children. I discovered that I had an idea in my head about what I thought my marriage would be like:

- I'd marry a single, career man about my age.
- I would feel comfortable in my own home.
- I would have equal decision-making power about the lives of the children living under my roof.
- The children living in my home would be my biological children.

- My husband and I would both experience things such as buying a house, getting a pet, or having a baby for the first time together.

Not once did I think "When I get married, I want to marry a divorced man with kids. I want to walk into a family that has already been created so I feel like I'm starting out already behind the curve. I want to feel left out and have to hold my tongue. I want to have to schedule our family calendar with another woman. Boy, does that sound like fun! Sign me up!"

You get the idea. Now go for it from wherever you are in the relationship. Let it all go. Don't be shy. Don't be a good girl. By all means swear if you need to. Get it out.

In order to extend yourself to these children and this man who are now or are about to become your family, you simply must know yourself. You had to learn about the industry you're working in, right? You may have spent years studying for your chosen field. When you join a stepfamily, whether you grew up in one or not, it's essential that you study yourself. You must be able to figure out why you have a meltdown when you have one. Ask yourself what is behind the freakouts. Are you upset that he was married before? Are you sad because a part of a childhood dream is dying? Are you denying that his old life has any power over your emotions?

It's okay to feel pissed off at a 5-year-old. Get it out on the page. Beat on a pillow or scream into it. If you tend to seethe rather than spew, try setting a timer and sitting down to write without lifting your pen from the page. Experiment. Then you can face up to what you're feeling and begin to analyze it. Imagine as you're writing that you are spilling all the emotions out of your body and on to the page so they do not reside within you anymore. Allow yourself to feel. If you're the kind of person who needs to detach a bit to get to your feelings, try using your journal for field notes. Be curious about what you're witnessing around you and within you in your new situation. Then get the hell out of the house. Get a massage. Go shopping. See a girlfriend or skip out to a movie in the middle of the day.

Fantasy of the Firsts

Once upon a time there was a man who fell in love and married a woman who wasn't you. They bought their first house together. They got their first pet together. Then they had their first baby and life was good. But then it wasn't good anymore, and they got divorced.

Then came along number two. Yes, that's you.

But number two just doesn't sound or feel so good.

Cheryl is a self-employed speaker and educator with a talent for inspiring business owners, executives, and employees. She's an avid jogger, canoeist, and cross-country skier. She is also effectively a stepmom of four adults. She met her partner, David, when she was in her thirties, and though she and David have never married, now at age 53 she's been with him for eighteen years.

When she looks back, she can pinpoint the moment she

first felt what it meant to be the second woman and how she dealt with that blow to her fantasy of her new happy relationship. "We had moved into our house and we like our house and we think it's special, but David said, 'I want us to keep a low profile.' He said he didn't want it to look like he was showing off, but that made me feel like I was supposed to be less than his first family and his first wife, and I said I don't intend to be second to anyone. I'm not here to lord our relationship over anyone else, but I am not interested in being treated less-than. I didn't cause their breakup. I am the result of their unhappy relationship."

Cheryl perceived that because she was not the first wife, she didn't rank as high, and she dealt with it straight on, confidently and matter-of-factly. As a professional adept at helping others work together, she used the skills she developed as an entrepreneur to establish her rightful place in her partner's life, without sacrificing her relationships with her stepchildren or the other household.

As the human resources manager for a large medical products company, Darcy honed her people and problem-solving skills and brought them home with her. "First identify the problem. Why does it happen? Then you take steps to resolve it and look for alternative solutions. You find what makes the most sense." When she married Jud, a man eight years her senior who was divorced with two kids, ages 7 and 11, instead of allowing her fantasy of being a first wife make her feel bad about her second-wife status, she identified her problem and then chose an alternative solution to help resolve her struggles at home. Darcy decided to be grateful.

"I knew when I got married at twenty-six years old that I would have two stepchildren. I knew that all my friends were having these fairy-tale weddings and didn't have to worry about an ex-wife and two kids. But I have a man who went through the hell of what a divorce can take you through. I am married to someone who appreciates what he has, who appreciates family and traditions because he knows what it feels like to have it taken away. His ex-wife said to me, 'You married a different man than I did.' Because now he understands what it's like to be hurt. I call Jud my diamond in the rough."

So what first-time fantasies do you have? Some topics for you to reflect on: wedding, first home–buying experience, honeymoon, first pet, children, holiday celebrations. But don't just dredge up angst and leave it there. Do something with it. Work out how it makes you feel and think of ways you can learn to deal with it or let it go. Like Darcy, find alternative solutions. Instead of dwelling on the jealousy or hurt, describe the wonderful experiences you have together, now, in the present.

On our first wedding anniversary I focused on all the wonderful memories I have of our magical day—not the fact that Arne's had anniversaries with someone else in the past.

We married on the beach at my family's cabin. Arne's three kids sat in the front row, and at the end of the ceremony they came up for a group hug. As Arne and I walked back up to the house, my stepdaughters, in adorable pink dresses, and my stepson in his navy blazer and khakis, led the rest of the attendees as they blew bubbles for us to walk through. It was a magical weekend our families still talk about.

When Arne and I returned to the cabin for our first anniversary, we looked at our wedding photos and remembered all those wonderful moments. Arne suggested we read our vows to each other on the beach, and we did so, on the same spot we were married. After that we shared the letters we wrote to each other that included reminiscences of the past year and our hopes for the future. No, it wasn't the first time he had a first wedding anniversary, but it was his first anniversary with *me*.

Yes, your man was married before, but he's never been married to *you*, so this partnership is a brand-new entity that has never been seen anywhere before.

Instant-Family Funk

Another common fantasy is that everyone will get along smashingly and every person in the stepfamily will have the beautiful happy family they've always dreamed of having. The kids will be perfectly behaved lovelies who will always kiss their new stepmother good night and tell her they love her. They will always mind her when she tells them to take their elbows off the table.

Dad will sit back and watch his new family with pride and relief, glad that he has repaired the damage he's done to his kids during his divorce. He can relax now that his children appear to be adjusting well to their new lives. After all, now they can witness a good relationship and not a bad one, and that's good for the kids, right?

Family vacations are fun. There are no meltdowns or tantrums. Everyone shares equally in the work, and all members of the family feel included and loved. After all, everyone got along before the wedding.

But many women find out that once the wedding day arrives, things change. No matter how well she got along with the kids before she and their dad walked down the aisle together, marriage triggers emotions in everyone—fear, anger, sadness.

Allison, an entrepreneur who was single for ten years before she met her husband, Charles, describes what happened to her after her wedding day. "Since I had never had children of my own, I was looking forward to the stepmom experience," says Allison, who gained three stepchildren when she married for the second time in her mid–forties. "Little did I know it would be full of land mines. Little did I know that when kids have no room to vent their anger, hurt feelings, sense of responsibility for the breakup of the marriage; when they can't rail at their parents for all the hurt they feel, partially due to divided loyalties between the two parents—guess who gets to step into the position of target?"

You got it. Stepmom. She's not related by blood, so all that anger and frustration can be more easily directed at her.

At the same time this stepmother was having fantasies about how everyone would welcome her into the family, the kids were most likely experiencing the death of their own fantasies, which might have looked something like this: Mom and Dad really aren't getting back together again. I really will have to live in two houses. My dad doesn't spend as much time with me as he used to. My dad is a different person when his new wife is around. I have to follow all sorts of new stupid rules. She can't tell me what to do. She doesn't even know me!

Debra jumped right into the coparenting mix when she started dating her husband Jake, who had two young daughters. As a marathon runner and driven career woman who traveled the globe for her job in medical device sales and later product management, she was a pro at targeting goals and achieving directives. She attended school conferences and basketball games and read the girls stories before bed. But when the engagement became official, all hell broke loose. The girls, who had treated her like a fun-loving aunt up to that point, were suddenly crying all the time, refusing to help out around the house, and waking up several times in the night to come bang on their bedroom door.

When her 7-year-old stepdaughter refused to try on dresses for the wedding and threatened to wear sweatpants, they began having family meetings so the girls could talk about their feelings about the upcoming nuptials. Eventually her stepdaughter became excited about participating and the wedding day turned out beautifully. But during that traumatic time, Debra and her soon-to-be-husband began seeing a counselor trained in stepfamily dynamics. And Debra joined a stepmom support group so they could be realistic about what to expect from their new family life.

There's really no avoiding the instant-family funk, which could also be called "transition" or "a whole new world." Any transition from one stage of life to another is going to bring up as much trauma as it does excitement. Think about moving out of your childhood home, going away to college, learning your way around your first job. The first six months working for any new company is horrible until you learn the ropes and figure out where you stand. So give yourself a break. This is a major transition. And it's going to take time for it to feel normal and comfortable.

All in a Day's Work

When you lived alone in your beautiful house or apartment with all of your lovely things just so, the maintenance really wasn't that big a deal. Maybe you did a little daily declutter and a weekly sweep of the house, perhaps a load of laundry on a Sunday afternoon or Tuesday evening. The dishes never stayed in the sink, or if they did, they were yours, so you didn't care. You didn't have to have arguments with anyone about how you ran your house. Things just worked out.

Part of the sparkling shiny newness of early romance is the fantasy that everything will just work out in your new stepfamily. And that means a lot of stepmoms don't take a moment to think about what it's going to be like living with a bunch of other people on a daily basis. They don't think about the work that entails. The responsibility it takes to raise children. The extra dirty clothes, the groceries, the disgusting ring that appears around the bathtub, or the unbelievable messes and odors kids can make.

For me, the death of one of my fantasies had nothing to do with the work involved, but instead it was about what that new responsibility represented to me—the death of my youth. I realized I was responsible for maintaining a household with children who lived in it 50 percent of the time. I transformed from a Miss to a Ma'am, seemingly overnight. It took me a while to figure out what was underlying my resistance to buying a notepad with a magnet on the back to put on the refrigerator for the grocery list. Even though Arne and I talked about the need for a magnetic notepad the day we moved in together, I didn't buy one until nine months into our marriage, after I had come to some acceptance about my new role as the female head of a household.

When she married her former high school sweetheart two years ago, Heidi gave up her job as a family law attorney to become a stay-at-home stepmom to her four stepchildren who range in age from 8 to 14. "I didn't think I had that many fantasies because I was a family law attorney. I know this can be ugly and hard. I have a sister who is a psychiatrist who told me I was crazy to do what I'm doing, but I had no idea how much work it would be."

Heidi had no clue what it meant to live with children. Her fantasy died when the reality of daily life revealed itself after she moved in with her husband and his brood. "I was constantly picking up," Heidi says of the many accoutrements of a child's life—the toys, clothes, dishes, backpacks, and books.

There will be things you'll have to discover as you go. Some fantasies won't crop up until you smack into them head-on. It was some time into my marriage when I finally realized that part of my vision of stepmotherhood was modeled on Julie

Andrews in *The Sound of Music*. I would come in to care for these children. I would sing and teach them lessons and smile all the time. We would all get along and harmonize beautifully. I would be the epitome of grace, kindness, and eternal patience, a far cry from Cinderella's wicked stepmother.

Because so many of the fantasies you hold about your family life will not reveal themselves right away, the best thing you can do is talk openly to your partner. And if you're not married yet or don't want to get married but plan to live together, you still need to have these conversations. The fact is, things will "just work out" if you take the time to build a relationship that will support you and your partner. The sooner you get everything out on the table, the better.

"Be clear about what your future spouse is asking of you," Gretchen warns. She's the vice president of operations at a marketing company with clients all over the globe and an ace at communicating with other people. "You have to talk about a hell of a lot more when there are kids and ex-wives. You better find out what you're dealing with. Being in love is easy when all you're doing is staring at each other. You've got to find out what they want. My husband wanted me to be an active parent. And you have to be honest with yourself about whether you can handle it. It's real. That ex-wife doesn't go away. People have to know that even though your husband and his ex are not married anymore, they are lifelong companions. I had to accept that this woman would be in my life."

Gretchen had few illusions about what her husband's or her own expectations were when they married, because they had so many conversations about it at the beginning. By using the communication skills that helped her rise up the ranks at work, Gretchen was able to face up to the realities of what it would mean to marry her partner, help raise his two kids, and manage his ex-wife.

Because giving up fantasies is so painful, it takes guts. If you need help, get it. And above all, spend time with your beloved. Whenever you finish a particularly difficult exercise, write down all the things you love about your husband. Talk to him and reminisce about the moment you met and your courtship story. Fantasies are great for daydreaming about, but reality is so much sweeter. You can reach out and touch him. Isn't that better?

DISCUSSION TOPICS FOR TWO

1. How do we picture our family a year from now?
2. Do we think we'll all get along? Do we want us all to love one another?
3. Do we want this marriage to heal everything from the past for us? For the kids? Is that realistic?
4. When we hit bumps in our relationship, can we work them out together as a team? Do we feel that we can face tough issues together? With the kids, the ex, the extended family members, the community? Are we both willing to get professional help?

5. Can we make our marriage our first priority, even though sometimes we might have to put the children before our own needs and desires?
6. What are the things we do really well together?
7. Can we create a new dream with goals we want to attain as a couple? As a family?
8. What is our definition of a family? Of a stepfamily?

CHAPTER 2

What Is a Stepmother?

Uncovering Your Expectations

CAREER GIRL'S PERSONAL ASSISTANT

1. Evaluate your performance. How would you describe your relationship with your stepchildren today?
2. Set benchmarks. How will you measure success?
3. Review assumptions. After observing the family you've joined, do you need to update your assessment of how each member is responding to this new formation?
4. Provide feedback. Can you talk to your husband and stepchildren about what it's like to be in their family? Can you tell them what you need?
5. Be receptive. Can you listen to your new family and hear what they need from you? Can you let them influence you?

* * *

Most resources for new stepmoms advise unearthing your expectations, but how can you figure out what your expectations are until you live them? How can you find your role in your stepfamily until you share a home with the people who will help you define it? Several studies have found that one reason stepmotherhood is so difficult is the ambiguity of the role. With no set cultural description of a stepmother besides the ever-popular wicked archetype, it's hard to find our place. It's tempting to immediately jump into a role of nurturer and caregiver, which leads some women to overreach their emotions and their authority before the relationships within their stepfamilies are built.

Anne O'Connor, the author of *The Truth About Stepfamilies*, was a single, newspaper journalist who covered the crime and education beats before she went freelance and married a man who had full-time custody of his 5-year-old son. "I didn't realize what a big adjustment it was to make. If I could help anybody, it would be that person getting into the relationship. You have to realize just how much you have to learn. I thought I was being very slow, very steady, and very smart. I wanted to be clear about what we were doing in our relationship before we dragged my husband's son into it. But until you start living with people and your life is affected on a day-to-day basis, you can't know how you will react."

I made sure I was as educated about stepfamily life as possible before I married Arne, even though I grew up with a stepmom and stepdad. I had a stack of books by my bed. Still, I felt tightness in my chest every time I thought about how much I had to learn. It was much like the early days of starting my own company when I had to learn the ropes of running my business. I knew it would take a while to figure out where I fit in with this previously formed family.

And yet after all the reading I did on stepfamilies and the mining of my history with both my own families, I was still dumbfounded by the many assumptions I didn't even know I had.

For instance, one night my then 10-year-old stepson, who is a sweet and sensitive kid I connected with immediately, came home with a dark cloud on his face. I assumed it was because he was upset about something related to the stepfamily. I went into problem-solving mode and wondered about all the ways I could help. I thought he was having trouble adjusting. My expectation was that his negative behavior was due to his pain from the divorce and his mom and dad's remarriages and that it was my job to help him, since I'd been there myself. It was a humbling moment for me when the problem turned out to be much more simple—he told me he hadn't slept the night before because he had sunburned his shoulders, and the heat and pain had kept him awake. After a full night of sleep, he was bright and chipper.

Examining your own background is a great place to start looking for where your ideas have come from about how things "should" be. If one of your stepkids comes into the kitchen and states "I'm hungry," and that makes you angry but doesn't faze your husband, it could be that you have an expectation that all children should say "please" and "thank you" just as you learned to do when you were a child. Your family of origin has a great deal of influence on how you behave with your new family—as Heidi, the family law attorney turned almost-full-time stepmom realized when she married her husband, John, and moved cross-country to be with him and his family.

Though Heidi tried to imagine how much her life might change, she didn't know what it would be like day-to-day until she moved in with John and his four kids after living alone for twenty years. "The house was a mess; the kids had no structure. The way I was raised was so different. That surprised me, how much I reverted back to how I was raised." While she missed her friends and family, looked for a job in a new state, and adjusted to an entirely different lifestyle, Heidi stayed home with the children the summer after her wedding while their father worked. In the middle of a job interview, Heidi realized staying home to help raise her stepchildren was more important to her than going back to work right away. Now, running the house is her job.

Her expectations about her role as stepmother had to do with creating normalcy and safety in the household. "I just decided, 'I am going to improve this situation, because it's not good.'" She was frustrated when changes wouldn't happen fast enough or the children resisted her as she implemented rules such as a regular bedtime. "I was just trying to make their life better," she says.

But she realized after she repainted the walls of the home most of her stepchildren had lived in since birth that perhaps she was pushing too hard. "The first summer together I was home with them a lot," Heidi remembers. "I thought I would find a full-time job, but I was pretty overwhelmed. I was re-painting the house, which wasn't so great for the kids, as the family therapist later told me. The kids complained. I was so hurt, but I had destroyed all of their memories even though I had let them pick colors and involved them. Later, they really felt a sense of loss and I could finally understand why they would feel that way. But at first I thought, 'Those ungrateful kids!'"

Many stepmothers feel the urge to "make things better" for their husbands and stepchildren, who have lived through a hurtful divorce or the death of a parent. It's understand-able, but it's important that a stepmother knows this expecta-tion can cause huge amounts of friction. If your stepchildren's mother is deceased, please consult with a counselor. Though this book will help guide you through stepmotherhood, the death of a parent brings up issues not handled here.

Lynn, formerly a communications expert at a Fortune 500 company, who has since received a degree in family services and started a stepfamily coaching business, remembers the difficulty she had managing her expectations when she first married a man with three children, two of whom lived with them. "I was so blind. I had these expectations that I was going to come in and make everything better. I think it was about eight months in and I said, 'I can't do this anymore. I need to go back to my old life.'" It was only after a meltdown about the pressure she was feeling trying to integrate into a new family that Lynn could identify what was going on. She would have to readjust her expectations—not lower them but change them.

It's tempting for stepmothers at the breaking point to lower their expectations to where they disengage emotionally from their stepchildren. That's where trouble can set in, because it directly affects the marriage, which in the early years is the weakest link in a new stepfamily. Because in any marriage, when emotional distance sets in, it's hard for partners to turn back to each other and back to the marriage.

My stepmother, Nancy, is the president and CEO of a national nonprofit association. She didn't have children of her own when she met my father. She put it this way: "Think about the common situations where parents are constantly on the run, bundling the kids off, getting groceries, helping with homework. If you have not come from that kind of lifestyle, and you suddenly step into it, you've got no time to adjust. To take that on is very risky. That's where the resentment builds. That's when people look for escapes elsewhere, by either working too hard or having an affair because they're so overwhelmed and scared."

Too much disengagement means you stay disconnected from your family, but there is a healthy amount of emotional distance for stepmothers. If you throw yourself in too far, too fast, you can also get in trouble. Georgianne, a consultant for a luxury car manufacturer, became a stepmother to four children ranging in age from 8 to 15 when she married her husband, T. J., at 43 years old. She had lived alone for thirteen years prior to that. She's an independent woman who loves to spend time alone and she catered to those qualities by choosing a career as a consultant so she can work in her home office.

At the time of her marriage, her stepchildren all lived with their mother three hours away, but six months after the wedding, two of the children asked to move in full-time with their dad. For the next three years, Georgianne took care of those kids while her husband, who worked long hours, was away.

"We got married in February 2002, five months after we started seeing each other. We are both pretty grown-up and knew what we were looking for. It didn't seem at all ridiculous, but then to be saddled with kids so quickly stopped the development of our relationship."

At first, Georgianne threw herself into the job of parenting the two children who came to live with her and her new husband. "The first year I was really game and gung-ho about it. I cheerfully drove to soccer practice. I went to fundraisers at school. But all of a sudden I realized, 'This is crazy.' I am the primary breadwinner in the family. I outearn my husband three to one. I can't be counted on for all of this. I was the one who got called by the school and had to go running if a kid missed a bus or they didn't do their homework. My husband changed jobs and was working even more, and I was left holding the bag. I was here with them on the weekends taking care of them when I should have had time off. I finally sat my husband down and said, 'Our marriage is suffering.'"

Part of the issues Georgianne and her husband were facing revolved around expectations: what her husband wanted her to do and what she expected herself to do. After three years of living with Dad and Stepmom full-time, the children moved back in with their mother. "It's not because they are not loved here or wanted here, it's because I can't be expected to make those sacrifices for them. It's mostly because my husband wasn't able to step up to the plate and take responsibility. It's disappointing to me that this was his solution: 'It's not working so we'll send them back to their mother.'"

No More Mr. Mom

As Georgianne's story illustrates, it's not only your expectations about your role that are affecting the daily tension levels in your home. Your husband has his own set of ideas that are influencing his behavior, too. Perhaps he believes that this new family will assuage some of the guilt he feels for putting his kids through divorce. Maybe he thinks you should just step in and become a mother figure for his children. Full-time stepmothers often report that their husbands expected them to step into the role their ex-wives vacated by asking them to take over the scheduling and school visits. A lot of dads hope for instant love between stepkids and stepmoms.

In psychologist Dr. Ann Orchard's research for her study, "Expectations of the Stepmother's Role" published in 1999 in the *Journal of Divorce and Remarriage,* she found a majority of the stepmothers she surveyed did not expect to replace or compete with her stepchildren's mother. But a large number of fathers expected their new wives to immediately take over the mother role and asked them to get involved in parenting, in effect replacing one family with another. Clearly, this can cause major disagreements in a new marriage, when the two heads of the house have such different dreams for their new family.

Heidi, the former family law attorney, now stay-at-home stepmom, remembers when John came to pick her up to move to her new home. As they neared their destination, her fiancé casually mentioned he would be out of town for four days with one of his boys at a Cub Scout camp program and she would have to stay home to care for the other three. He assumed she would be okay with that arrangement. Though she was uncomfortable with it, she did as he asked. She remembers the summer after she and John married as one of the most challenging times in her life.

"My husband would come home, and thank gosh for his sense of humor. He would ask me, 'Who are you today? The babysitter? The maid?' It was hard for me. But I actually am glad we had that time because the kids and I bonded. It was so intense; it was do or die for us. We had to hang tight together or we wouldn't have lasted. I could have taken an adversarial role, and they could have. But I felt like I had to do it."

Debra, the medical device product manager and stepmother of two young girls, says she and Jake stayed up arguing one night about the kids when they had lived together for about six months. The wedding was only a few months away, and daily life was in turmoil as the household culture already in existence clashed with the culture Debra had acquired from her family of origin. They fought about how one of the girls wanted to sleep with them in their bed, and Debra thought that at age 7, she was too old for it. Jake felt guilty about saying no, especially when the girl would lie on the floor in front of their bedroom door. Finally after going around and around for hours, they got down to the underlying issue.

"I do not love your kids," she whispered. "I might never love your kids."

It hurt Jake to hear those words from his future wife, but he was able to listen and respond. They were able to discuss how both of them felt differently for the children living under their roof. Debra was virtually a stranger. There was no way she could feel the kind of unconditional love for those girls that her husband felt. And even though her husband could understand her viewpoint, he still hoped that they could be one big happy family.

"The love I have for those girls is not unconditional; it's conditional," says Debra, whose sentiments echo many of the feelings expressed by stepmothers across the country when they are first struggling to form a new family. Bonds between steps can become strong and long-lasting, but it doesn't happen overnight. And it doesn't happen for everyone.

Sandy was 36 and an established account manager at a media company when she married her husband. Tim had two boys, 8 and 10 years old, who lived with their mother and stepfather in another state. The only time Sandy's stepsons spent with her and her husband was holiday vacations and five weeks every summer. For Sandy, it was like a bomb erupting in her house every time her stepsons arrived because it was such a disruption to her and her husband's daily lives. And though she never once let on to her stepsons, with whom she has very close relationships now that they are 17 and 19, she admits she sometimes hated their guts.

"It got to the point that I thought, 'I hate these kids. I wish they would run out into traffic. I wish they were never born.' And then I felt evil and rotten and was sure I was going to hell. Then I thought, when they come here for the summer, I am going away. I'll go stay in a hotel down the block so I don't have to be here. The minute my stepsons walked in the door, my husband would drop our life together. It resumed when my stepsons left."

One of Sandy's expectations was that her relationship with her husband would remain important even when her stepsons were around. But because this dad saw his sons so infrequently, when the boys were in town, their entire lives revolved around them. It didn't help that Sandy and Tim have never gone on a trip together after nine years of marriage, because Tim uses all of his vacation time from work to visit his sons or take time off when they're in town.

Eventually, Sandy realized she would put herself into a panicked frenzy as the time neared for her stepsons to come for their annual summer visit. When they actually showed up, it was never as bad as she had told herself it would be, and they all had fun together sightseeing or hanging out on the back porch talking.

"We're buddies. Sometimes I'll take a couple of days off and my stepsons and I will have the whole day together. I love to go through art museums and I'll drag them along and they pretend they enjoy it." The more Sandy started telling herself they were going to have a great time, the easier the summers became. But even now that she's been in a stepfamily for nearly a decade, she's aware that it still hurts Tim to know she will never feel about his sons the way he does. Expectations are closely linked to fantasies, and it can be quite painful when you have to accept that some of them won't come true.

Where Do I Fit?

As you've begun the work of identifying what everyone in your stepfamily unit feels and wants from their family experience, you can begin to solidify what your role will be with your family members. "I didn't always know what I was doing," admits former family law attorney Heidi. "What is my role? What are my boundaries? I think the kids were looking to me for boundaries, but I didn't know what they were. How far do I go in deciding how this house is run now that I'm here? How far do I go in asserting myself or trying to fit in?"

To find out what role best works for you and your family, you must first sit back a bit and observe. Being a stepmother is an identity that evolves over the course of your lives together, so keep your eye on the big picture. You've got to work your way up the family ladder.

Let the kids tell you what they want from you, and see if that fits with what you're willing to give. Because there are no known models for what a successful, generous, kind, and involved stepmother looks like, you get to create a role that fits with your own temperament. As time goes on, you and the kids will negotiate with each other until you arrive at workable relationships.

Some possible positive roles for stepmothers are trusted adviser, teacher, friend, coach, and respected adult. Psychologist and author Patricia Papernow called the role "intimate outsider," in which you are close and part of the family, but you are also just a bit outside so you have a more objective viewpoint.

Your role is also going to depend on what ages the kids are when you marry their dad. Children's behavior changes as they move from one developmental stage to the next. A younger child is going to be more open to hearing, "Sweetie, can you pick up your toys?" than a 10- or 16-year-old.

When I was a teenager, I was angry and rebellious. There was no way I would accept direct parenting from my stepmother. To do so would have put me in a direct loyalty conflict because I believed if I let her influence me, it would hurt my mother. For several years I said "No!" to every suggestion my stepmother made, regardless of whether I thought it was a good idea or not, simply because it came from her.

Even though our relationship was rocky at the start, there were topics I talked to my stepmother about I would never have brought up with my mother or father, such as boys and sex. Her perspective on the world added value to my life.

Now, my stepmother has created a place in my family that is entirely her own, and she is no less a member of the family than any of us. Isn't that what it's about? Each of us has to declare space in our families for our unique personalities and contributions, no matter how we came into the family. Each of us is responsible for every one-on-one relationship we have with our parents, stepparents, and siblings, and that interaction is what makes a family. You'll find your role. It will grow organically out of the ingredients of your own unique situation.

Free to Be Me

Here's an exercise designed to help you see what your comfort zone is, to help you figure out what kind of stepmother you want to be. Consider the statements as jumping-off points, and if something rings true for you, follow it and see where it leads.

- I want the kids to be able to talk to me about their problems.
- I don't want to feel responsible for their daily lives: their schooling, discipline, friends, allowance, guidance, etc.
- I want to be an active participant in their daily lives.
- I am an affectionate person and I love it when they give me hugs and kisses.
- I want to tuck them into bed and read them stories.
- I am more comfortable remaining at a distance, like a teacher who gives guidance but does not get emotionally involved.
- I do not need my stepchildren to give me emotional support.

- I want my stepchildren to make me feel loved and included in this family.
- I can tell them what to do, like pick up their socks or dirty dishes.
- I want us to be respectful of each other.
- I want to be the ringleader of fun.
- I want to be a role model.
- I want to feel like they're my kids.
- I want to be a mother.
- I have never wanted to be a parent.
- I have no idea what I'm doing, but I'm willing to be open and accepting of my new experiences.
- I'd like to be a warm and soothing influence on my stepchildren.
- I want to be the "intimate outsider."
- I want to feel that I am a part of this family.

Figuring out your role within the stepfamily is a lifelong process. You, your husband, and the kids will negotiate it over time. You can create the role that fits for you and your family.

Empowerment

In many of the resources out there for stepmothers, there is an abundance of "woe is me" tales that can inspire dread in the hearts of even the most stalwart of women. The horror stories of stepmothers tortured by teens gone wild, vindictive exes, intrusive former in-laws, and wimpy spouses are all true. It's important to be realistic about what you can expect from stepfamily life. At the same time, if you start your stepfamily with the assumption that your life is going to suck for the next couple of decades, you can be certain it will.

So the challenge is this. Explore yourself. Take the time to figure out what you feel. And don't be surprised if some of this exploration takes you to some icky places. Stephanie is a stepmother of one boy who was 12 when she married his father, Luke. Stephanie was in her forties, had never been married, and was highly accomplished in her career as a college English professor. "I had all the strategies; big deal," she says of her struggles with her rebellious stepson who acted out by getting involved early with sex, alcohol, and drugs. He began staying out all night at 13 years old and would often steal jewelry from Stephanie and money from his father. "We're all smart, aren't we? But they trigger all your own emotional stuff."

Those emotional triggers are wrapped around deeply held dreams, fantasies, and expectations, all of which have implications for your ability to find your place within your stepfamily. Stephanie advises stepmothers to delve deep into the work of personal growth. "I want to encourage people to do their work—and I don't just mean housework. Do the hard spiritual and emotional work it takes. Ask: What is the meaning of this? Figure out why you're here and what you're going to contribute."

DISCUSSION TOPICS FOR TWO

Talk openly with your husband about your role within the family. Both of you need to express your views and arrive at something everyone feels comfortable with.

1. Do either of us know any stepmothers? What role did they appear to have in their families?
2. What have we each imagined a stepmom's role to be in our family?
3. How do we want the children to think of or behave toward their stepmom?
4. What do we think a stepmother should be willing to give? Do? Share?
5. How much of the daily responsibility of raising children should a stepmom have? Driving to day care or school? Shopping for groceries?
6. What kind of authority should a stepmom take on? Getting kids to help with dishes? Sending them to their rooms when they're bad?
7. Should Stepmom be required to take care of the children when Dad is not around?
8. Is it appropriate for Stepmom to be involved with the communications between Mom's house and Dad's house?

CHAPTER 3

Face the Music

Getting to Know the Kids

1. **Gain market intelligence.** What do you know about children? What is your experience to date with kids?
2. **Learn the ropes.** Before you attempt to parent your stepchildren, ask yourself this: Have you taken the time to build a strong relationship with them?
3. **Gage your responses.** If your reactions to the children's behavior are emotional, can you identify the underlying expectations fueling your response? Are you competing with the children for Dad's time and attention? What would happen if you cooled off for a few days so you could look at the situation in a new light?

4. **Networking opportunities.** What things can you do to get to know your stepchildren? How can you sell yourself to them without them (or you) feeling like a used-car salesman?
5. **Problem solving.** What things can you do to create the most positive atmosphere possible in your home?

The first time I met my stepmother, Nancy, my two younger brothers and I thought it would be funny to bring along a whoopee cushion. The plan for the evening involved dinner and a movie. We raced ahead of the adults to find seats in the theater, and before she sat down in the half-darkness, we slipped the cushion onto her seat.

I looked straight ahead at the screen as she entered our aisle, trying to act as normal as possible and not crack an evil grin. It couldn't have been more perfect. She had no idea. She hadn't seen us blow up or plant the giant pink plastic farting toy on her seat, and she sat down hard. The sound echoed through the theater, and my brothers and I laughed our little heads off. Though we all thought it was hilarious and it helped break some of the tension, the truth was, we were scared of her and it made us feel as if we could exert some power in a situation in which we had none.

She describes that day from her perspective. "I clearly remember my own feelings of anxiety, and even terror. I may have revisionist memories, but I vaguely remember seeing the whoopee cushion before sitting on it. I wanted to go along with the gag. I thought it was endearing for you to do something, even something mischievous, to welcome me. Something naughty was better than nothing at all. A laugh was better than silence."

I waited a month to meet Arne's kids, and I wanted to meet them so they became real to me, instead of being just the idea that "Arne has three kids." I was terrified when I drove up to the suburban house where they lived. That moment in the theater meeting Dad's girlfriend for the first time came back to me, and I felt sick. What did his kids have in store for me? Would they try to embarrass me in front of their father? Would they hate me? Would we get along?

It took thirty-five minutes to drive out to his house from my apartment in the city, and it was like driving from one country to another. The skyscrapers gave way to shopping malls and newly developed neighborhoods. I even drove past a few farms with grazing horses and cows. When I pulled into the driveway, I had to take deep breaths to center and calm myself. I saw chalk drawings and discarded bikes on the pavement in front of the three-car garage. When I looked down at my hands, they were shaking. I felt as if I was walking into an interview by committee for the biggest job of my life.

When I entered the house, they were all sitting at the kitchen counter in a row eating lunch.

"This is my friend, Jacque," Arne said. He introduced his two daughters and his son, ages 3, 5, and 8, and I managed a twitchy smile. I think I said, "Hey, guys," or something equally cool and noncommittal. Immediately lunch was forgotten, and they jumped up to gather around me. I was surrounded by a gang of attention-seeking humans all anxious to show me their rooms, their favorite toys, their latest drawings. It appeared they were not armed with a whoopee cushion, handshake buzzer, or can of slime to throw at me.

After several hours spent playing together at a nearby park, we sat down to dinner. The children moved constantly, chewing and chatting. Arne's son told me facts about the *Titanic*, his middle daughter talked about her best friend who lived down the street, and the youngest girl said she could jump all the way across the room on one foot. Arne tried to get them to behave, to eat slowly, to remove their elbows from the table. And I sat shell-shocked. I smiled and answered questions. I ate the food my date prepared for me, but there was a part of my mind that had gone numb from the overwhelming shift in my world. I didn't know quite how to be, how to act.

My gaze fell on the refrigerator, which was plastered top to bottom in photos of the kids and pictures they'd drawn. I thought of my own fridge at home. It was covered in magnetic poetry that formed sentences you wouldn't find in any children's book. I felt as if I had landed on another planet— one I knew absolutely nothing about.

Then I thought about those kids, and the new world they were living in, one they didn't have any control over at all. At least I had choices.

No matter how a kid approaches you at the beginning— open and willing to get to know you or hostile and wary— you've got to remember that kid's world has just been completely upended. Everything that child has ever known has changed, and he or she may be operating out of fear, confusion, and deep sadness. The divorce of their parents will affect them for the rest of their lives, and you can have a big impact on helping those kids succeed.

Asset Assessment

You might be used to running the show at work, but when you start a job, you must learn the culture before you can be effective. You know when you take on a new client it's going to take time and work to get to a place where you trust each other. Why, then, would we assume that when we join a new stepfamily, it's going to turn into a strong and bonded family overnight? Your stepfamily is going to take years—that's right, *years*—to bond. So try on this mantra for size: Slow and steady wins the race. Slow and steady wins the race.

When you build relationships with a new friend or co-worker, you spend time alone. You go out for lunch. You ask them questions. You get to know what they like and don't like. In return, you share yourself so they come to know and trust you, too.

It's the same with your stepchildren, with an added bonus: They have experienced a trauma, and so their relationships with you could be loaded from the get-go. In the beginning, your most powerful tools are to listen and learn. Find out who your stepchildren are. What do they like to do? What are their favorite colors? Who are their best friends?

Most stepfamily experts recommend that a new stepmother should not begin parenting a stepchild right away and instead should chill out for a while, especially if the kids are adolescents. If you take a new job in which you are oversee-ing other people who have loyalties to the person who vacated your position, you know you must assess what everyone's role is before you can begin to assert your own. You first interview everyone and find out how things have been working before you begin implementing changes. It's the same with stepfam-ilies. So take time to gather information before you demand allegiance from the kids.

If you have more than one stepchild, it's easy to fall into the habit of treating the kids as if they're in a pack. Some-times that pack is friendly and will come up to you for pet-ting. Sometimes it's a big snarling mess that can tear a new stepmom apart with belligerence and anger. Set up one-on-one time with your stepchildren and you'll be more able to accurately see their personalities and assess their individual needs.

"Don't treat all the kids as a clump," says Jeff, a grown step-son in his thirties who grew up in two high-conflict stepfami-lies. "They are all individuals. Everyone will react differently to the divorce. One will be mad and the other will be sad."

Cosette is a stepmother to three children and has been married to their father, Paul, for twenty years. She and her husband are both marriage therapists and run a private prac-tice together. Cosette laughs as she says owning a business with her husband has been harder to do than creating her stepfamily, but she's not kidding. Her warm and compassion-ate approach to her stepchildren made it easier for everyone.

As a therapist, Cosette has had plenty of practice helping people open up about their feelings and really listening to their needs. She applied those same empathetic listening skills that made her so successful at work to building her relationships with her stepchildren. She remembers that as she got to know her stepkids, she let them each tell her what kind of relationship they needed from her. "I got to know them one-on-one and they each made an effort. That was the key. They weren't 'The Kids.' And they were all so hungry. They love their mother, but my stepson would just talk and talk and talk. I would need to change clothes and he would keep talking through the door. He was very open and they were all willing to just know me."

By spending time with your stepchildren, you can begin to see your family's personality. It becomes easier for you to understand what it must be like for the children to have a new woman in their lives, and you can then consciously begin to craft your plan for the future.

Of course, Dad will have to get out of the middle and let you develop your own relationship with his children. "I was never pushy about acceptance," says Jenna of her four step-children, ages 6, 8, 13, and 15. The kids had just watched their parents go through an ugly divorce and still struggled with loyalty issues when their parents said negative things about each other. "I never had any kind of preconceived notion that I would replace their mother. I figured the relationships would develop the way they would. I've always been a kid person and I play a lot so that made it easier. We played and had fun and I didn't put pressure on the relationships. At first my husband Carl's expectation and desire was that I would come in and the kids would love me right away. I knew that wasn't fair. The relationships would evolve or they wouldn't. He put some pressure on, but I wasn't ready to be serious right away."

When Arne and I went through our premarital counseling with my aunt, Debbie, a Lutheran minister who officiated at our wedding with her husband, my uncle, Steve, who also is a pastor, she told Arne he would have to allow me to be a part of his children's lives—that he couldn't get in the middle because he felt guilty about what he was bringing to the marriage. She reminded him (and me) that I was an adult and had made the decision to be with him, fully aware he was bringing three lovely children to the relationship. It was my choice. And he had to respect me enough to let me live with my choice. Then he had to let us all get to know one another on our own terms without jumping in to protect me from them, or them from me.

Getting to Know You

As I began building relationships with my future stepchildren, I wondered if the skills I'd learned at work could help me become a better stepmother. For my job on a magazine staff, I learned how to interview by asking open-ended questions. I learned how to make people feel comfortable with me so I could get the information I needed for a story. As a reporter, I had to be curious about every person I interviewed, while remaining objective enough to be able to accurately report about their lives. Plus, I had to be organized so I wouldn't miss a fact or state an incorrect or incomplete thought. I spent more than a decade learning my craft and with every "Good job!" and promotion, my confidence grew.

When I met Arne's kids, I used my training as a journalist to get them to open up, to investigate their likes and dislikes. Because I put myself into a situation in which I didn't feel comfortable, since I hadn't spent much time around kids, I naturally fell into using the talents I did feel confident about to help me find my way. You're an accomplished woman with on-the-job training that you've spent years perfecting. So what special skills can you take home from work that can help you get to know your stepchildren?

What you will have to do to begin establishing relationships with your stepkids is largely determined by their age and gender. If you have a stepson who loves going to the movies, ask him what he wants to see and make a date of it. Go to lunch beforehand or get an ice-cream cone afterward. To avoid making a child feel that you're bribing him or her with treats, don't just buy things. Make the outing an experience—something you can both do together that allows you to have time to develop your relationship. It could be as simple as walking your dog around the block or taking your stepchild grocery shopping.

"Have stepmom-stepdaughter time," says 15-year-old Nicole, a teenage stepdaughter who likes her stepmother, Kathleen. She met her stepmother when she was 6 and is

now an eloquent teen who explains why she and her stepmother get along so well. "Find something you both like to
do together. We both like coffee shops. We both like movies.
Spend an afternoon doing things you like together."

When there is a lot of hostility from a kid, it usually springs
from years of history that a new stepmother may know nothing about. The best way to find out if you're walking into an
explosive situation is to talk to your partner. Find out how his
previous marriage ended. Listen to how he talks about his
ex. Ask him about the kids. Have they exhibited any behaviors that would indicate they're having a tough time? Watch
how your spouse coparents with his ex. Do they dump things
on the children to deal with because they can't talk to each
other? For instance, does Mom tell the kids to collect child
support payments from their father? If so, you could be in for
a rough ride.

The children will also give you an idea. Listen to the clues
they give you about things going on in the other house, but
never make a judgmental comment about their mother's
house. This is tricky because you don't want to ask directly
how things are going at their mom's. Children will automati-
cally respond by defending their mother. This is extremely
challenging territory. It's usually best to get as much information as possible from your partner and practice your listening and observing skills with the kids to make sure you're
in the know.

"You've got to remember that it's not the kids' fault," says
Eleanor, a former New York City chef-turned-midwestern
stepmother of two boys she met when they were 2 and 7.

"Usually when kids say something horrible, they are prompted by the adults. It's the adults that mess it up, not the kids. I think we are the ones in our insecurity that pump the negativity right down to them."

If you were involved with their dad before the end of his first marriage, the child might make you the target of all his anger and pain, because it would be far too painful to blame his father for hurting his mother and breaking up the family. Another factor that could influence a stepchild's behavior is the length of time she lived with her single parent. If a kid feels like a parent's confidant or protector, a new stepparent can make a child feel threatened in that role, no matter how old the child.

Andrea is a successful marketing executive. Her parents divorced when she was a preteen. Even as a young adult, Andrea felt threatened when a new woman entered her father's life, because she was "Daddy's girl." Her father didn't remarry until she was 25. Andrea, now 30, remembers slamming the door in her new stepmother's face and rejecting all her advances. When Andrea became a stepmother of a 9-year-old girl, she could finally empathize with her stepmother. Now Andrea and her stepmother are close friends.

I Spy a Kid

See if you can answer these questions about each of your stepchildren. If you can't, take your stepchild out for a soda and see if you can fill in more of the blanks.

1. Favorite color?
2. Best friend?
3. Favorite book?
4. Favorite band?
5. Favorite movie?
6. Favorite game?
7. Is your stepchild allergic to anything?
8. How does your stepchild spend time after school?
9. Who is your stepchild's teacher?
10. What is your stepchild's favorite class? And why?
11. Do they have ideas of what they want to be when they grow up?
12. What types of games do they like to play?
13. How well do they do in school?
14. How would you describe your stepchild's personality?
15. What would you say are your stepchild's most admirable qualities?
16. What do you like to do with your stepchild?
17. In what ways has your stepchild opened up to you?
18. What do you think your stepchild needs from you?
19. What are your stepchild's fears?
20. How does your stepchild feel about Dad?

All Aboard

You know if you're planning a new direction for your department, the rest of the people in your company have to go along with it if anything is going to get done. The same goes for the other people involved in your new marriage. You are not just marrying this wonderful man you met—you're also binding your life to his children's lives.

"I think if you get married, it's a pretty good idea to get buy-in from the kids," says Jeff, whose parents each remarried within a year of their divorce. "Both of my parents got married knowing their kids hated the people they were marrying. Maybe more communication on the front end would help the dynamic, because once it's set, it's set. You don't want the kids to feel like their opinions are discounted and marginalized."

A majority of remarriages occur within two years of a divorce, and so the children are still working out their grief and fear about their parents' divorce when the new couple gets together. That makes the work of building a strong stepfamily even more difficult. You and your future husband have to weigh for yourselves how long you're willing to wait to get married, but factor the children into your decision. Consider where your soon-to-be stepchildren are in their grieving process. You might as well get used to thinking of them, since they'll influence all of your decisions from now on. If the children are particularly antagonistic, be real about the difficulties your marriage will face and commit yourself to creating the strongest bond you can with your spouse.

My husband and I married a year and a half after we met. That was probably too soon, but we were in love and wanted to be together. The kids kept asking us when we were going to get married and we figured we would deal with any fallout after the fact. It was difficult to be patient because we were just so excited to find each other. But we couldn't expect the kids to be as excited about our relationship as we were. In fact, our wedding pictures tell the story.

The body language of one of my stepdaughters radiated sadness. Typically, as the middle child, she is outgoing and talkative. If there's a camera around, she's sure to have a smile and a special pose for the photographer. When our wedding photographer snapped a picture of her during the ceremony, her head was dropped forward. She was looking down at her hands, which were tightly clasped in her lap. Her feet were tucked up and nearly covered by her tea-length pink dress and her toes were turned in toward each other. While all the people around her smiled, she had a frown on her face. She looked as though she was trying to become as small as she possibly could.

That day was the start of my dream and the end of hers. As of that moment, there was no hope her parents would get back together. When I looked through those pictures after our wedding, my heart broke for that little girl. And it's my job as an adult to recognize her feelings and be as empathetic as possible. It's not that little girl's responsibility to make me feel comfortable joining her family.

I have a picture someone snapped of my brothers and me at our dad's wedding to our stepmother. They had flown us all to New York City for the wedding. In the picture the three of us are walking away from the photographer down a busy city sidewalk. I'm 13 and my brothers, ages 11 and 9, are on either side of me. We're all holding hands. That photo gives me such a melancholy feeling, because I remember how sad and scared I was that day. Life was going to be very different for us from that moment on. And we had no idea what to expect.

Even for stepmothers who hit it off with their stepchildren, the wedding day can be an emotionally traumatic event for a kid. On the other hand, sometimes the kids are the ones who push for an official ceremony.

Mary is a nurse. She and her husband, Pat, chose not to get married at all until her stepchildren were grown. She met Pat when she was 32. At the time, he had full custody of five children between the ages of 3 and 9. Mary was happy with her single life and was in no hurry to move in with anyone, so she and her husband dated for eleven years before they married. She maintained her own house and her single lifestyle until the youngest was in high school. When she finally did get married, the kids helped plan the wedding, insisting on making it more extravagant than even Mary had planned, because they were all so excited to finally officially have her in the family.

It Takes Two

As Heidi, the former family law attorney, found out when she first moved in with her four stepchildren, it was exhausting for her to be at her best all the time. "As I got to know the kids better and they got to know me better, we were able to have downtime together," she recalls. "At first I was always 'on' with them. I was attentive. I felt like I had to actively take care of them. Now I can be home with them and they can do something other than what I am doing."

As they all relaxed into their relationships, Heidi found out she needed to let the kids get to know her as much as she worked on learning about them. Now, one of her favorite things to do is to sit around the kitchen table after the kids have come home from school. They all have a snack and each person talks about their day—including Heidi.

Cosette also worked hard to open up to her stepchildren and stepgrandchildren. "I consciously tried to be real with them," she says. She often passes along the lessons she's learned to other stepmothers she sees as a marriage and family therapist. "I find a huge mistake people make is when people get married and then immediately try to exert their authority. You can get them to mind you, but the way you win out in the end is when they know who you are and they respect you. They might even grow to love and appreciate you and that's where your power comes from. You can't demand love; you have to earn that. You have to walk carefully and let the relationships grow."

Sandy, whose stepchildren come to visit every summer, also felt it was important that she be herself. "I was never mean, but I was never too nice," she says. "I tried to truly reflect how I was feeling. Sometimes I would play with my stepsons, but when I didn't feel like it, I wouldn't fake it. They got it, and so I learned it was okay to be me. I was so worried. But they want me to be me if I'm mad or sad or happy. They want to know the real me, not some paper-doll image of me. I've always tried to be myself. It's so tiring to be that nice, sweet lady all the time." Her dedication to being herself paid off. Now that her stepsons are teenagers, she has a positive relationship with them both.

But don't expect your stepchildren to take on the responsibility of asking you about your life. As I got to know my own stepchildren, I let details about my life slip in as we talked about things we had in common. Because I have two step-families that are still together after more than two decades of marriage, I introduced my stepchildren to my families. They welcomed the kids with open arms and demonstrated for them what having a binuclear family looks like.

When I'm in a bad mood, I try to let them know I've had a long day and I'm tired so they don't take my behavior personally. If you are a stepmother who is always on, always defensively combating the wicked-stepmother myth, you rob yourself of real relationships with your stepkids.

Code Red

There are a couple of relationship deal-breakers for kids. Though every family situation is unique, it was remarkable how many times I heard stories like this one:

Brooke's parents got divorced when she was 2 months old. Her father remarried when she was 9, and at first she didn't have any problem with her stepmother, whom she never lived with. "It was always playtime," she remembers of her visits to their house.

But all of the warm feelings they were developing changed

in an instant when her stepmother felt that she had to protect her new husband from his daughter. "I forgot my dad's birthday one year, and when I finally called him, she screamed at me. That instance had a huge impact on me and that was probably fifteen years ago." Since that moment, their relationship has taken a nosedive.

No kid wants to feel that her father needs to be defended from her, especially early on, when a relative stranger to the family is doing the defending. It's the kiss of death for many stepmother-stepchild relationships. Just as Dad shouldn't get in the middle of your relationship with his kids, in the eyes of the child, you have to stay out of her relationship with her father and respect it. They have known each other longer than you and your husband have been together. Your man needs to handle his own relationships with his kids.

The second deal-breaker is when a stepparent tries to discipline a child too early in their relationship. In Brooke's case, she felt that her stepmother was trying to lay down the law when she hadn't done the work of building a strong relationship with her first. On the other hand, she allowed her stepfather to tell her what to do because he was the one cheering her on at all of her games and concerts and helping her with her homework every single night. He had earned the right to parent her.

If you've done everything in your power to avoid a Code Red and the kids still don't like you, take comfort. Children can learn how to manipulate a situation to best fit their needs. Believe me, I did. They bring their own opinions and behaviors to your relationship that influence just how close you'll be able to get, no matter what you do. There are plenty of stepmothers who eventually create positive relationships with difficult children, but it could take years of patience and compassion. It's the same with biological parents and challenging kids. My own parents say they thought I was a jerk for most of my adolescence, while I rebelled by breaking rules and sassing all the adults in my family. Yet we're all close now. So don't give up!

Stepfamilies That Play Together

Whether you're meeting your stepkids for the first time or planning activities together as a family, try to engage everyone. But you can't take it personally if a kid doesn't want to participate. If one stepchild decides to sit it out while the others play, find out what the party pooper likes to do and do it separately. In the meantime, if he sees everyone else having fun, he just may want to join.

Games

Game night is a long-standing tradition known for its bonding power. Gather everyone around the table, grab a deck of cards, shuffle and deal, and you'll have hours of fun with time to talk built in.

Walkabouts

You don't need a dog to get out for a walk on a beautiful day, though a pooch certainly makes a convenient excuse. As my youngest stepdaughter said, "I love going on walks with the dog because me, you, and the puppy get to be alone." We also like to go on walkabouts on weekend afternoons where we explore different parts of our city on foot. All you need is a backpack, a bottle of water, a camera, and a couple of bucks for a treat or spontaneous museum visit along the way.

Sing-Along

If you're musically inclined, a sing-along is always a fun bonding experience. When we do dishes after dinner, we turn on the *O Brother, Where Art Thou?* soundtrack and yodel and dance around the house to bluegrass music as we wipe down the table and put away the placemats.

Judy's stepfamily all sang and played instruments, so they harmonized together, especially in the car.

And years later I still remember the silly song my stepmother taught me on our weekend trips to the family cabin about Madelina Catelina, a poor disfigured woman. The song catalogued all of her ailments, including this one: She had two teeth in her mouth, one pointed north and the other south.

Movie Marathon

Gretchen, her husband, Brad, and her two stepchildren would rent an armful of movies they all wanted to see and have movie marathon nights. "All little kids want to know they can stay up as late as they want," Gretchen says. "So we would stay up as late as we could, sometimes until two or three A.M." Now that her stepdaughter is 21 years old, she still comes home from college and asks if they can have a family movie night.

Dinnertime

Judy, her three stepchildren, and husband, David, bonded over meals by using the red plate. "We would designate one person to receive the red plate, and the plate says, 'You are special today.' We would articulate what we appreciated about whoever received the plate, and they would say what they appreciated about themselves. It became a tradition to appreciate each other in a formal way."

Holidays

There are few things in stepfamily life more stressful than holidays. But this is where the beauty of successful stepfamilies really shines. In research by John and Emily Visher, pioneers in stepfamily research, and the founders of the Stepfamily Association of America, they discovered that stepfamilies who were able to come up with creative solutions and adapt to the fluid nature of stepfamily life were most successful. The holidays are the perfect test to see just how flexible your stepfamily is.

If your husband and his ex insist on splitting every holiday right down the middle so the kids have to schlep from one house to the other in the middle of Christmas Day, for instance, consider how disruptive that is to the kids. Why not be creative and really see the spirit of the holiday you plan to celebrate? Who cares about the calendar date? Many stepfamilies have solved the issue by holding separate holidays on completely different weekends, or if possible, both sides of the child's binuclear family gather at one set of parents' house so everyone celebrates once and together.

Believe me, your kids will thank you someday if you make the holidays easier on them. Then you can enjoy one another and plan to spend a day exactly the way you all envision it together. Find out how everyone in the family wants to celebrate and you'll make all members of your family feel included.

Get It on Paper

Another great way to get to know your stepkids is to write letters. One year, my father insisted that we all write Christmas letters to our family members that described the past year of our lives. We were asked to include our achievements and disappointments and our dreams for the coming year. Then on Christmas, when we all gathered, we read the letters out loud to one another.

For the first several years that we did this, it was a torture session as we all worked through old pain. There were always several tissue boxes on hand. And though it certainly wasn't fun all the time, eventually it became clear that those letters helped us to know one another and bond as a family.

Cheryl, who became a stepmother to three grown children with children of their own, made her stepgrandchildren feel included in her busy life by sending them postcards every time she traveled anywhere.

Allison was a successful entrepreneur with her own interior design business who met her husband, Charles, when she was in her mid–forties. He was in the process of getting a divorce after twenty-seven years of marriage and had three kids ages 12, 18, and 19. At first, Allison's relationship with her stepchildren was turbulent.

"When we got married, I sat down and wrote each one of the kids a letter," she says. "And I think that letter paved the way for our strong relationships today. I wrote each one a letter based on each child's needs and personality. I told them I was lucky to be a part of their family and that I loved their dad tremendously and hoped that we would always have a happy relationship together.

"I told them I knew I wasn't perfect and that I would make mistakes and that I needed for them to tell me when I was doing things that distressed them or hurt them in any way because it was not my intention. I told them I would never lie about anything, and if they wanted to know something about me or my family or career, that my life was open to them. I would tell them anything they wanted to know. I said I would do my best to be a good wife to their dad and that I hoped they might someday feel comfortable coming to me for advice. Finally, I said I would never assume that I would be in the position of being their mother. Now, ten years later, they say those letters meant more to them than anything."

Allison says her relationships with her stepchildren have deepened over the years. "I have grown to love them so much," she says. "I even get Mother's Day cards from them and regular e-mails. They come to me with their problems and they value my opinion. Our lives are so rich. As controversies arise, we know how to handle them. We *are* a family."

DISCUSSION TOPICS FOR TWO

1. Are the children open to a new relationship with Stepmom? How can Dad support those new friendships without getting in the middle?
2. What fun things can we do together as a family?
3. How can we support the kids in their transition?
4. What can we do to make time for each of us to have one-on-one outings with the kids?
5. What have we learned from the kids?

6. Where can Stepmom's parenting contribution fit into our unique family dynamics? What kind of guidance should Stepmom offer the children?
7. How can we support each other's parenting styles so Dad doesn't feel criticized and Stepmom doesn't feel completely left out?
8. What are some wonderful things about the children? Where do we see the kids headed? What kind of adults do we think they will become?

CHAPTER 4

. . . .

From Sassy Single to . . . Wife?

Learning How to Be Married

CAREER GIRL'S PERSONAL ASSISTANT

1. **Appraise communication skills.** Pay attention to the words you say to your spouse, especially in an argument. Are you able to really listen and understand each other?

2. **Employ negotiation.** How well can you both hear each other out and then come to an agreement that feels fair to both of you?

3. **Build your team.** What are you doing to promote team building between you and your partner? What combined cause do you have?

4. **Exercise strengths.** How do you plan to fortify the foundation of your partnership? What things do you already do? What would you like to do?

5. **Celebrate achievements.** It's important to consciously mark your milestones. What large and small celebrations can you plan together?

There are so many things to do before you walk down the aisle to your beloved groom and his kids. You have to figure out the wording of the invitations and decide if the children will participate. You must choose the location, music, flowers, caterer, and fashions. As all brides know, there are plenty of magazines, books, and websites out there to help guide you through the planning process. But rarely in bridal literature will you find the number one biggest thing you must do: You have to learn how to be married.

If you've lived alone for a long time, moving in together can be a rough road. When my husband and I first moved to our house with his three kids, I had a legendary meltdown, now known to my family and friends as the "Pants Incident." I walked into our bedroom and there was a pair of Arne's khaki pants on the bed. With all the stress and strain of moving from one kind of lifestyle to another, it was, for me, the breaking point. And though I am embarrassed to admit it, I flipped out on my poor husband, asking him, "But what do the pants *mean*? Am I supposed to pick them up or leave them there? Are they clean or dirty? Do you expect me to do something with them or do you expect me to try and ignore them? What do the pants mean?"

Since then, I've come to understand the meaning of the pants. They were a marker for me, a signpost announcing that I now lived with someone else who would influence my physical and emotional space. Learning to do the dance of partnership is a lifelong endeavor. The good news is, there are tools to help us learn how to be married.

Within the last decade, a marriage education movement has picked up steam in this country to combat divorce rates, which, though they have begun to decline in the last few years as more people choose to cohabitate instead of marry, still hover around 50 percent for first marriages and 60 to 70 percent for remarriages.

Every year thousands of relationship and family professionals gather in June at the Smart Marriages conference held in various cities by the Coalition for Marriage, Family, and Couples Education, an organization based in Washington, D.C., that advocates healthy marriages through education. Marriage and relationship heavyweights such as John Gottman (*The Relationship Cure*), Pat Love (*Hot Monogamy*), and John Gray (*Men Are from Mars, Women Are from Venus*) are only a sampling of the pros who attend and speak at the conference to figure out how to help people make their marriages last. The many talks and classes put on during the weeklong event center on the fact that educating couples about married life leads to healthier relationships.

The idea is that if you learn the skills you need to make your marriage run more smoothly, such as making each other a priority, compassion, communication, and conflict resolution skills, you'll better weather the ups and downs of married life.

Learning how to live in partnership with another human being is an exercise in humility and personal growth. When there are children involved, the temptation is to put the kids before all else, including your marriage. But the trouble with that model is that the couple relationship, which is the most fragile bond of the entire stepfamily structure, is destroyed when it's sacrificed repeatedly for anyone else, whether kids, in-laws, or colleagues. That man is the reason you're in this stepfamily, and your relationship with him has to be strong. It *cannot* be the weakest link, or the entire family will disintegrate. Tell your husband I said that—and I can back it up with research by *all* the top stepfamily professionals.

Here's a common story. When Sandy married her second husband, Tim, he had two young sons. "If my stepsons and I were both drowning, my husband would save his kids and I would be shark food. That's really disturbing. You hate yourself for thinking that, because they're little kids. When I talked to my husband about it, he said, 'Well, I would save my sons because I figure you could save yourself.' But that's not what I meant."

Sandy needed to feel that her relationship with Tim was as much a priority to him as it was to her. She wasn't confident in their commitment to each other at that point. Though some research does say that a strong marriage is difficult for stepchildren to watch in the early years, eventually it is your union with their father that, if made a priority, can provide them with the stability they may be sorely lacking.

In a partnership, each member has to feel equal. But in

a stepfamily, the primary partnership has so many strings attached that one partner sometimes gets pulled off to one side, leaving the other feeling vulnerable and betrayed.

My father, Ron, remembers how his wife, my stepmother, Nancy, struggled as a formerly single woman with three new stepchildren when her fantasies of her new life met the reality of day-to-day life. "She has Prince Charming and here come the beasties. They arrive and tear apart her dream, her castle. And they are doing it in the worst possible way. They are taking away her Prince Charming because suddenly he's not on her side anymore. And that's one rule for Prince Charming—he stays on your side no matter what. All of a sudden you've got a 7-year-old who turns him into a talking head that says to his wife, 'Now, honey, you're the adult here; let's be mature.' So the marriage goes into immediate jeopardy when those realities hit."

So how can a couple stay on each other's side in an environment where that seems almost impossible? People who feel confident and accepted are far more able to face challenges. A woman who feels secure in her marriage is far more likely to be flexible when a child's needs have to come first, as they often do. I recall a day when my husband and I had plans to go out for lunch because we hadn't had any alone time in ages. Then he called to cancel because my stepson had pinkeye and had to be picked up from school. I was disappointed, yes, but I knew that his need to help his son did not affect our relationship to each other. I knew I couldn't begrudge him his duty as a father, and I also knew we would reschedule our lunch for another day. But it's easy to see that if I hadn't felt that my husband valued me, I would have felt jealous and angry that our plans to spend time together were interrupted.

Allison, the entrepreneur, remembers how challenging the first few years of her marriage were to a man with three teenaged kids, until she and Charles refocused on making their relationship strong. "When it was Dad and the kids, the old family dynamics were online, and they didn't include me in any way," Allison says. "In the beginning, they made a point of not including me. They'd tell family jokes, have family discussions about family trips and holidays and presents they'd unwrapped. There were times at the dinner table when literally not one person would address me, not even my husband. Even though I was taking up a chair, I didn't exist."

The first year of her marriage was so tough that Allison and Charles nearly divorced. "I had to sit myself down and say that my primary focus had to be on my husband and our relationship. I knew I could become a twisted sister with all of the things going on with the kids, but if I focused on what I could do to create a solid relationship between him and me, then we would survive."

Sounds pretty grim, doesn't it? Especially when you consider what a single career gal gives up to join a stepfamily. Space that's all her own. Money she can do with as she pleases. Time to hang out with friends or spend as she sees fit. Freedom to come and go without having to make plans with a babysitter, husband, former in-law, or ex-wife.

The negativity surrounding a new remarriage doesn't help you get off the ground with the same buoyancy of a first marriage. When I said yes to Arne's marriage proposal, I heard the same phrases from all of my married acquaintances: "Marriage is hard enough without stepkids. Good luck." Or my favorite, "You're either really stupid or really brave."

Excuse me?

One of my colleagues launched into a monologue about how she had dated men with children, and she told me she gave me credit because, by God, she would never do that again. Another friend said, "Well, honey, it's going to be hard, but if anyone can do it, you can." We'd all dreamed over lunch breaks or brunch or Cosmos about when "he" would show up and how wonderful it would be. Yet when he did show up, I was showered with negativity.

That pessimism about marriage, combined with a lack of education about how to be married, puts you one click away from divorce.com. How can you succeed without a glimmer of hope that your marriage will be enjoyable and fulfilling?

I propose that having fun in your marriage has to be just as conscious a choice in the early stages of stepfamily development as the discussions about money. When you've just given up that sweet loft apartment you had in the city or the quaint little bungalow you finally just found that last perfect piece of furniture for, and instead find yourself picking up the most disgusting-smelling socks from the middle of the living room floor where your stepson left them, you're going to need a lot of positive feelings about your marriage to counteract the nasty odor.

Marriage researcher John Gottman, cofounder of the Gottman Institute in Seattle, has come up with a mathematical equation for couples. In his research, he found that successful couples had a ratio of five positive interactions, such as compliments or loving touches, to every one negative interaction. Think about that. If you start your stepfamily life mired in thoughts of how difficult it's going to be, how can you rise above the anger and hurt aimed at you by wounded kids who can't direct it at their parents? I am all for being realistic about what's coming. Indeed, you've got to be able to recognize the stepfamily dynamics that play out in the lives of remarried couples. But that doesn't mean you should abandon hope while you're at it.

Rules of Engagement

Conflict is just part of the deal when you're in a relationship with another human being who does things differently than you do. Madeleine L'Engle wrote a beautiful poem to her husband of thirty years that is in her published journal *The Irrational Season*. I don't know that the poem even has a title, but I call it "You Are Still New," and I read parts of it to my husband during our wedding ceremony.

In the poem, she describes the feeling of knowing this man so intimately for so long, and yet, still, he is a stranger to her. She could never see the world through his eyes, just the way he sees it. And therefore he is still new to her. I thought the poem was humbling. It addresses the incredible responsibility you have when you're in a relationship with another, who will always see things differently than you do. It also means there will be conflict and negotiation and compromise.

You have a choice about how you behave within your marriage. Your husband does, too. The old saying "Familiarity breeds contempt" is based in truth, and yet there is nothing more corrosive to a marriage than contempt. Gottman says he can predict with more than 90 percent accuracy whether or not a couple will divorce by watching how they deal with conflict. A couple is in trouble if what Gottman calls the "four horsemen" show up: contempt, criticism, defensiveness, and stonewalling. But he says that contempt is the most damaging of them all. The lesson: Learn how to fight fair. Learn to listen to how you speak to your spouse. Be civil.

My Aunt Debbie, the Lutheran minister, suggested that my husband and I make a Rules of Conflict list during our premarital counseling sessions. We made a list that has fun rules as well as serious ones based on both of our personalities. Our list of rules looks like this:

1. No silent treatment.
2. Time to think—thirty minutes or more.
3. No fighting in front of the children.
4. No running off in a car in the middle of an argument.
5. If one person is not ready to talk and has been clear about that, the other person can't push discussion.
6. Come to some resolution or agreement to continue the discussion before bed.
7. Always say, "I love you," and kiss good night.
8. Never start arguments with "You always" or "You never."
9. If no resolution, thumb war or rock-paper-scissors.
10. Must conclude argument with makeup sex.

11. No starting arguments just to have makeup sex.
12. Be nice.

We printed out two copies of the rules, one for my desk and one for his. And we've pulled out the list in the middle of arguments to keep us fair and on track. The reading of the list makes us laugh and helps to dissipate the tension so we can have a real discussion about the issue we're debating instead of an emotional tug-of-war. That last rule is perhaps the most important.

P. M. Forni is a professor at Johns Hopkins University in Baltimore, cofounder of the Johns Hopkins Civility Project and author of *Choosing Civility: The Twenty-five Rules of Considerate Conduct*. He says this is the advice he has for couples:

1. Think of yourself as a good and accomplished person who does not have to prove your worth all the time.
2. Exercise restraint.
3. Practice empathy.
4. See your spouse as an end in himself rather than as a means for the satisfaction of your immediate needs and desires.
5. Defend yourself from toxic stress because stress causes uncivil behavior.
6. Do not shift the burden of your insecurity onto your spouse in the form of hostility.
7. Before acting or speaking, ask yourself, is this merely self-serving or is it the right thing to do? Do this, for example, before asking your spouse for a favor.

8. Consider the consequences that the action you're about to take will have on your spouse.

9. Wonder whether for your spouse, your presence is preferable to your absence.

10. In a challenging situation, such as confronting your angry spouse, imagine that you're being videotaped and that your video will be used to train others in handling that situation. That way you can acquire a certain distance, a healthy detachment that allows you not to blindly yield to anger.

To-Do List

So how do you keep your marriage front and center even when you suddenly have children knocking on your door, interrupting private moments? No matter if you have your stepkids full- or part-time, you're going to need to make sure you and your husband spend time together developing your partnership.

In a first marriage, a couple typically has several years to work on becoming a team before a baby comes along to test their bond. You get no such time to feel confident in your relationship with your mate before you're launched into the thick of things. Your bond is immediately tested, before you've had a chance to define what it is. So it's crucial that a new couple consciously decide to make time together.

"Marriage is very difficult and you have to work on it every day," says Eleanor, the former New York City chef who moved to the Midwest. Her husband, Marty, has two sons from a previous marriage, and he and Eleanor have one son together. "I try to make sure that we are still a couple and not just parents. That we have private jokes. Learning how to be married was harder than adjusting to the stepkids."

As a single woman in a big city, Eleanor went where she wanted when she wanted. But she found that Marty was protective of her and didn't want her doing things such as walking alone at night. "He'd say, 'You can't go out in the dark,' and I'd say, 'What?' Then he'd tell me I should act like a married woman. I had to go from being a party girl to a calmed-down married girl. I learned I had to work at our marriage every day or it wouldn't work."

Here are some little ways you can make sure you continue to develop your partnership so you feel supported as you create your role as stepmother.

- Explore each other. Think of your husband as a new land you've never been to. Find out what makes him tick. Be interested. Be curious.

- Stay connected. Every morning and evening check in with each other. Have coffee together on the front porch. Walk the dog around the block.

- Plan things to look forward to. In bridal literature there's a time just after the wedding when the bride and groom both feel a sense of postwedding depression. After the drama and intensity of the months leading up to the big day, settling down into the nitty-gritty of everyday life with other people in your space can be a bit of a downer. So plan something else to look forward to. Plan a trip for your one-year anniversary. Plan big trips for your fifth, tenth, and twentieth anniversaries.

- Find things you love to do together, and do them. Go to the movies. Cook gourmet meals. Hike in the mountains. Go to a football game. Get involved in a charity you're both passionate about.
- Learn something new together. Go to a class. Make or build something.

One stepmom I talked to complained that her husband never planned their date nights—that she had to or they wouldn't happen. She bought the book *101 Nights of Grrreat Sex* by Laura Corn. The book contains 101 ideas for private events one partner plans for the other one, and her husband really got into the planning. Each chapter says "For Her Eyes" or "For His Eyes" and are sealed shut so no one can peek. Now they both plan nights together that have ended up making them feel closer to each other.

Many books about marriage refer to the need for open and honest communication, and it's true—it's crucial to learn how to talk about difficult things. However, those hard-hitting discussions must be balanced with fun. Remember Gottman's research? How many positive moments do you have every day? How many negative interactions?

After my husband and I spent an entire day working on our household budget and having several heated exchanges, we went out to our favorite art movie theater for a film we both wanted to see. Then we hit our new favorite wine bar for a glass of wine and dessert. The images I've retained from that day are not the time spent in our home office, but the time spent watching a great film with my love holding my hand. Plus, we actually worked through some financial discussions, so we felt as if we'd accomplished something big as a team.

Us Against the World

In a culture of self-interest, how do you turn "What's best for me?" into "What's best for us?" The challenge of any marriage is to figure out how to work and live in a partnership while maintaining your own purpose. But the only way to achieve a working stepfamily is if both you and your husband work together as a unified team. It's a process of trial and error, but one that must stand on the assumption that both of you are committed to supporting each other.

Consider Judy and David. They formed a stepfamily twenty years ago with her husband's two children from a previous marriage. And though there were challenges with the kids, it was her husband's parents who caused the biggest heartache. They formed an alliance with their son's ex-wife that excluded their own son and their grandchildren's new stepmother—Judy. It was devastating to both Judy and her husband.

"I wanted a really solid, open, dedicated, and healthy marriage," Judy says. "I wanted our relationship to be number one, and my husband agreed it would be number one for him, too. He never ceased to demonstrate that when it was critical. He demonstrated completely to me that he would do anything to preserve his relationship with his parents, short of undermining our relationship."

When my dad first married my stepmother, I didn't want to see outward signs of my dad's new marriage being healthy and strong. But eventually, the growing quiet strength of their marriage became something I could count on. It became something I could learn from.

Without that strong bond between the two of them, our stepfamily would have combusted long ago. So, stepmothers, besides working on your own inner strength, which is something we must all do, make that relationship with your husband strong. Be confident in it. Play with it. Make it yours. And then you can extend your open arms to those children from a place of security and strength that will help those kids flourish through the wounds of divorce.

DISCUSSION TOPICS FOR TWO

No matter where you are in your relationship with your honey—dating, engaged, married, or living together—there are things you absolutely must talk about. Before you sign a prenuptial agreement, you have to disclose to your soon-to-be spouse everything you have: all of your assets and debts. And he has to do the same. Doesn't it make sense then, that before you sign a marriage or cohabitation contract, you disclose everything you can?

The conversations you have with your spouse about your values and priorities are the building blocks for the foundation of your marriage. Create a structure for your partnership that will support your marriage in good times and bad.

1. What does being a wife mean? What do we expect from each other?

2. How do you expect life to change now that we're married? What do you feel like you'll have to give up? What things from your single life must you keep?

3. What happened in your husband's previous marriage? Why did it end? What is the biggest lesson he learned from his divorce?

4. What are our personal histories? What events have forged us into the people we are today?

5. What are our feelings about sex? Pat Love, the author of *Hot Monogamy*, spoke at the 2005 Smart Marriages conference in Dallas, Texas. This was one of her twelve road rules for a passionate marriage that she gave in her speech: "Have sex. Sex delivers. It's good for you physically and emotionally. Have sex because you promised to. How can you expect fidelity and monogamy if you're not a passionate partner?"

6. How were we both raised?

7. Do we want children together?

8. What will we do in the event of emergency? What are we willing to do to save our marriage? My husband and I wrote out an agreement stating what we will both do if our marriage is in trouble.

9. How can we create a combined sense of purpose? Marriage expert John Gottman thinks successful couples need to create a shared sense of meaning. What do we both strongly believe in? How does our faith influence our marriage? Do we both feel that giving back to our community is important? Do we have similar dreams of where we want to end up together? Does our partnership have a purpose?

10. How do we envision our partnership in five years? Fifteen? Thirty?

....

CHAPTER 5

This Land Is My Land

Day-to-Day Life in a Stepfamily

CAREER GIRL'S PERSONAL ASSISTANT

1. Review space requirements. Discuss living arrangements in advance with your partner. What kind of space do you need? What space does your husband need? Your stepchildren?
2. Analyze the existing structure. How do your husband and his kids interact with one another? How does he parent them?
3. Build community. The children will more easily accept your influence if they feel that you care about them. How will you make the kids feel that you're on their team?

4. **Strategize cool-downs.** If you see a behavior that drives you crazy and your husband doesn't correct it, you have a decision to make. Having a strategy beforehand can make those moments easier to deal with. Do you say something to the kids? Do you hold your tongue? Or will you talk to your husband about it later?

5. **Delegate authority.** Sometimes letting someone else do their job is the best thing you can do to encourage productivity. You can still have input, but you don't have to do all the work. Can you let your spouse parent his children?

Back when I was a sassy single gal in my late twenties living in my cool bachelorette pad, I remember my parents telling me to relish my existence. They knew that one day, when I got married and started a family, I would miss that apartment. I would long for the quiet and the orderliness. I would crave the serene, smooth sailing of my even-keeled emotions. They were right. Back then, even PMS would hardly cause a ripple in my calm because my environment was so entirely harmonious—and it was mine, all mine.

My home was perfectly arranged. Just walking in the door made me feel soothed. If there was a mess somewhere in the house, I had made it. But when my daily life suddenly included three children 50 percent of the time, things changed, to put it mildly. Where would all those dolls and trucks and toys fit in my feng shui map? How could I turn down the volume? My remote didn't work on the screams, laughs, or bickering.

When my stepkids, my husband, and I first moved in together, I felt as if I was in over my head. There were so many things I didn't know. For instance, I didn't know that you don't give young kids glass cups because they might bite them and break the glass in their mouths. Where would I have learned that? I felt dangerous because I didn't know what I didn't know.

As in the movie *Matrix*, I wanted an instant download that would teach me everything I needed to learn to be a wife and stepparent. I wanted to know right away what my role was within our stepfamily. How many rights did I have in my own house? What could I say to the kids when they were misbehaving and their father wasn't around? How much power did I have?

At one point very early on in our daily lives together, I stood at the kitchen sink angrily scrubbing the dirty dishes of five people and feeling like the hired help. I wasn't even angry because I was doing the dishes while everyone else was still sitting at the table talking. I was upset because I felt powerless to say anything if I saw a kid doing something he or she shouldn't, such as sneezing and wiping a nose on a sleeve or kicking a sibling under the table. And that made me feel invisible. The feeling was compounded every time the kids wanted to tell a story and always said, "Dad," to get the table's attention, even if they were looking directly at me.

At that point I hadn't yet found my place, and not knowing what I was *allowed* to do in my own home drove me nuts.

Debra, who admitted to her husband Jake that she didn't unconditionally love her stepchildren, remembers the moment it hit home that her lifestyle had changed. She was sick, and also in training to run a marathon only two days away. "We were going to bed and the younger one woke up with leg pains; she was sobbing and in hysterics. We didn't have any medicine in the house because we weren't very organized, so I had to go, at eleven P.M., to buy children's Advil. We finally got her in bed, and then at midnight her sister came in and said, 'I have diarrhea.' I remember sitting up in bed and crying. None of this is that bad—it's just, what about me? You know what I mean? I had this realization that, wow, I'm a parent, and it doesn't matter how sick I am, or what else I have in my life, this child has diarrhea."

Debra's oldest stepdaughter would accept her ministrations when she was sick—but as soon as she felt better, the little girl would do her best to make Debra feel like an outsider.

Stories like Debra's are exactly the type of experience stepmothers can't talk about with just anybody. Friends or siblings who have children have had time to adjust to what life is like with kids, and they don't understand why this is so upsetting to a new stepmother who was a complete stranger to these children not long ago. Biological mothers have a deep love for their children that balances the more challenging parts of parenting. Stepmothers are often expected to act like mothers in the daily running of a household, and that places them in a bit of a bind. First, they are not mothers. Second, they are new to parenting. Third, they don't have the same kind of emotional bonds to those children as the biological parent does.

Even without all of the emotional issues that can stack up on a stepmom's shoulders, the transition from living alone to living with a bunch of other people is enough to induce stress.

Allison entered her stepfamily when the kids were in their teens. Late one night she got out of bed and walked into the kitchen in the half darkness. She stepped in something, slipped, and fell. One of the kids had knocked a bowl of chili onto the floor and left it there. He hadn't bothered to clean up. It's a funny story for their family now, but it wasn't funny to Allison when it happened in her first year of marriage.

She remembers another story. "My house looked like an interior designer lived in it. And suddenly these whirling dervishes were living in my house! In *our* house. One of my stepsons ran down the stairs with his guitar and he knocked all the art off the wall all the way down the stairs, and then he left it there. He said, 'See you later; I'm running late.'"

Heidi remembers her former life. "I lived in my very own space for twenty years before getting married at 42 years old. And my house was the same in the evening when I got home as I left it in the morning." When she moved in with her four stepchildren, it's easy to imagine, that was no longer the case.

Sacred Space

We all need to feel as if we have a place to call our own. And to be the best stepmother you can be, it's crucial to lay claim to a space that can become your sanctuary, whether you're moving into the home where the kids already live (which most stepfamily experts recommend you don't do if you can help it) or you're all moving to a new place together. Then when the stress of daily life gets to be too much, you have somewhere to go.

Because I work at home, I knew I needed to have a home office that was off-limits to the kids. So when we were looking for a new house to move into, that was one of the priorities for us. We found a house with a room big enough to have my desk and workspace plus a couch if I needed to escape into the office for a break. My husband installed a lock on the door and told the kids they were allowed in the office only if I'm in it. The kids refer to the space as "Jacque's Office" and have been respectful about knocking.

A lot of women new to a stepfamily find it difficult to make their bedrooms off-limits to the kids because they feel guilty. If the kids are used to coming in during the night to snuggle with Dad, and they can no longer do it, they might resent a new stepmother. But boundaries are okay. Here's how Debra solved her bedroom issue. Her two stepdaughters were used to coming in every morning to snuggle with their father, Jake, and watch cartoons. After Debra got buy-in from her husband to make the bedroom their sanctuary, Jake got up to watch cartoons in the living room and snuggled with the kids on the couch. Everybody won.

When Mary finally moved in with her husband, Pat, whom she had dated for eleven years, she set up her boundaries as she went along. "My husband's room used to be the meeting place, so that really had to change. I freaked out one time because after eating my breakfast, I went back into the bathroom in the master bedroom and there was my stepson taking a shower. But that's what he was used to doing. And we didn't ever sit down and say, 'Okay, now that Mary's here, things will be a little different.' I wish we had talked over more things ahead of time, but when I moved in, I was so overwhelmed that we just never got around to it."

Georgianne had never been married before when she moved in with her husband at 43 years old. She was also the primary breadwinner in the family and worked at home. Her office became a no-go zone to her four stepchildren. "My office is off-limits. They can come bother me in my office if the house is on fire. They respect that boundary, but unfortunately, my office has become too much of a refuge. I always know I can get away from them when I go down there."

When Lisa, a corporate executive, moved into the house her partner, Liz, and her two children already lived in, Lisa admits she had to fight for her own space. "I had this beautiful three-bedroom town house with a family room, a dining room, a workout room, and it was all mine. Then I moved into a dinky little office. All my stuff went from a 2,500-square-foot house to an eight-by-eight room. I gave up a hell of a lot. And that has been very tough. I don't even have my own bathroom. It was a continual struggle to try to maintain some space. It makes my eye twitch just to think about it."

No matter how small your home is, do whatever you can to carve out a place that's just yours, even if it's just a reading nook beneath the staircase where you can put a chair, a light, or a little bookshelf. Feeling that you have at least a slice of something that's all yours, knowing you have somewhere to escape to, will help ease the grind of daily life.

You're not the only one who needs a room of her own. The kids need a place they can call theirs, and so does your husband. In our house, we have a third floor that is the perfect play area, library, and TV room for the kids and their dad. I don't go up there much because it's their space. And I ignore it when I'm cleaning. My husband enlists the kids' aid and they take care of picking up the third floor so I don't get involved. They know that they can go up there when they need to get away from it all. When I say good night to the kids, I do comment on how lovely and clean it is after they've picked up, and praise them for it, but other than that, I keep my nose out of it.

When you and your partner move in together, it's also a good idea to keep displays of affection in your sacred space. Your stepchildren will already pick up on the sexually charged atmosphere, especially if they're adolescents. Don't do any kissing or touching that will make them uncomfortable. If you've got a stepson in your house, don't walk around in a towel after a shower. Get dressed in the bathroom. If you are uncomfortable with a stepson who likes to bare all, enlist the aid of your husband to remind his son to keep his bedroom or the bathroom door closed when he's changing.

If you've got a stepdaughter, be respectful of how she

feels watching you touch her father. Holding hands is fine, but if you grab his ass or smooch him in front of her it could make her feel grossed out or worse, that she has to compete with you.

Transition Days

When the kids move from Mom's house to Dad's house and back, it is known in stepfamily circles as "Transition Day." When I was a kid, my parents didn't know there was a term for it, but I remember my mother commenting how crazy my brothers and I would all act the day we left her house for Dad's and the day we returned. We would be loud and energetic, running around the house like maniacs, or moody and somber. Sometimes we fought viciously among ourselves. And it was because we were transforming from the people we were expected to be in one house and becoming the people we were supposed to be in the other house.

Alex is a woman in her twenties, who grew up with a stepmother who was a career woman with no children of her own. She remembers the transition between houses as one of the most difficult parts of her childhood. "The hardest thing about having divorced parents was the huge difference between the two houses. At Dad's house we were expected to do our own dishes, and we would forget, because we didn't have to at Mom's. I was supposed to brush my teeth before breakfast at Dad's house but not at Mom's. It was hard having to remember.

"One of my stepmother's big things was that we couldn't bring clothing from her and Dad's house to our mom's house. The transition was always very hard to figure out. They knew the transitions were hard. Mom always had a routine for us. We would go put our stuff away and then have a certain amount of time to ourselves before dinner. We always did it the same way."

Like Alex, I had to adjust to the different rules and rituals at my parents' houses. For Christmas morning at Mom's, we all gathered around the tree to open presents in our pajamas with our hair still messy. None of us brushed our teeth; we just ran down the stairs to find out what Santa left. It was the same way we'd done it since we were old enough to walk. At Dad's house we had to get cleaned up and dressed before we were allowed to begin the holiday. That way we'd look presentable for photos. It doesn't seem like that big a deal really, but to us it felt like the rituals we were used to weren't good enough, and by extension, that *we* weren't good enough.

Children are smart. They'll figure out what the differences are between houses, but be aware that every change you make could make the kids feel that you don't approve of their mother or them. Don't be surprised if your stepchildren throw tantrums or act as if they've just eaten a pound of sugar the day they leave your house and the day they return. Alex's mother did a wise thing by giving her children time to acclimate to their new environment before she requested their presence at dinner.

Rule the Roost

When a stepfamily unit first moves in together, it's pretty easy for women to clench up and try to control everything in the household, including the children. But this is a mistake, ladies. Try to breathe and sit back. Watch the kids and find out how the house was run by your husband before you came along. You are the stranger in the house. And it's not your place to be disciplining the children right away or demanding that they clean their rooms and make their beds every day. It's your job to get to know them. Find out what rules they are used to living by.

"Stepfamilies are very different from biological families. People often go into a remarriage thinking that now they've found the perfect husband or wife and everybody is just going to blend together," says Michele Diamond, a licensed independent clinical social worker who specializes in working with stepfamilies near Boston. "It's not as though you put a woman and her husband and his kids from a previous marriage into a blender, press a button and it all comes out smooth. It comes out really, really choppy. The biological dad and the stepmom have to have really clear communication between the two of them. They must work together as a team. But the biological parent, especially at the beginning, has to be the one who sets the rules for the family."

Your husband must step up to the plate. He's got to take the lead on the parenting instead of just sitting back and letting you do it, especially in the first few years. "Dad's got to be supportive when you decide what your role is," says Patti Kelley Criswell, a licensed clinical social worker in Portage, Michigan. "If you say, 'I can't stand it—the dishes aren't done,' he has to be the one who says to the kids, 'Come on, guys, let's do the dishes.' He has to work hard. Stepmom can't run the house with someone else's kids. That's not fair, and that's months or years down the road. Should kids do dishes? Yes. That's not the point. It's not that you're wrong. It's just not your role yet. You're not family at this point; you can't declare that you're family. You grow into family."

Darcy, the human resources manager, agrees. "My advice to new stepmoms is similar to what I say to new hires at work. You take the first six months and you observe, you listen, and you appreciate. Then you can initiate and execute. If you don't understand and you don't listen and you're trying to push your agenda, it doesn't work. It's a process. You can't expect the kids to love you right away. You have to grow together and learn together and make mistakes together."

First, find out what the kids need. "It's different in every family," says Criswell. "Is there a bio mother around? If so, then you take on the role of the favorite aunt. What is Dad like? Can he parent? Or is he the kind of man who is looking for someone to do it for him? You have to earn it slow and steady with kids. Disapproval from a stepparent is like a bomb."

When you move too fast, too soon, the kids tend to have long memories. It took years for Alex to say complimentary things about her stepmother, whom she met when she was 10.

One of the most vivid memories from her childhood is what she calls Manners Boot Camp. "She was very strict. We would sit at the table to eat with my stepmother and Dad standing over us. They would watch us and critique us. They'd watch to see which forks we used or if we chewed with our mouths open." Today, Alex and her stepmother accept each other, but they are not close.

"The hardest thing about parenting a stepchild is that you don't know what you don't know," says author and stepmother Anne O'Connor. "You don't know how you're going to respond in a situation. How much are you going to rock that boat? No matter how much you disagree with how parenting is happening when you get there, you have to be respectful of how they are parenting that child."

Telling Dad he doesn't know what he's doing with his children can leave him feeling criticized and defensive. So tread lightly when you're having discussions with your husband about parenting.

My husband, Arne, describes the feeling. "Any time you have a new authority figure it's going to be difficult. It doesn't matter how much you love someone or trust someone. The first time you see your new wife reprimanding your kids, you're going to feel defensive. If you notice it, you have to talk about it because something like that doesn't go away all by itself. Acting defensive could be something a guy doesn't realize he's doing."

But you can expect to be treated with respect in your own home. "Dads really need to step up," says Criswell. "Their message to the kids needs to be, 'You can't call the shots, but you really matter. And I want everyone to be happy. This isn't about sticking you with a new stepmom to make you unhappy. Because I love you and I love her, I really want this to work out.' He is the coach. Nobody gets any direction without him. He defines how far the kids can push a stepmom."

Dad needs to retain the primary responsibility for his children, always. But Stepmom needs to feel heard and empowered, too. There's nothing worse than feeling that you're invisible or walking on eggshells in your own home, in the space that is supposed to allow you to relax and let the stress of the day run off. What most stepfamily experts recommend is that the couple sit down and hammer out a list of household rules together that Dad then presents to the kids along with what the consequences are when they are not followed. That way, you can feel included, but Dad still takes the responsibility (and blame) for the rules. Then Dad can say that the house rules are to be adhered to by everyone and that you, as another adult in the family, have the power to enforce them.

When my husband and I first moved in together, we tried to make the household rules right away, the first month we were in the house. We realized, however, that we didn't know enough then about what needed to be on the list. We had to live together a bit more to figure that out. Finally, after we'd all been together in the house for almost a year, my husband and I finished our list. It includes most of the items that my husband was already enforcing with his kids, but we slowly added a few that made me feel better about living in our house.

I'm a pretty laid-back gal generally, but I'll admit there are a couple of things that drive me crazy. And when I moved into a house with three complete strangers, who would leave their bags, shoes, toys, coats, gloves, balloons, papers, and garbage all over the living room and dining room, I would hyperventilate every time I arrived home to a space that looked as if it had been ransacked by robbers. It reminded me of my college days living in an apartment with a bunch of roommates who left their belongings out everywhere. Only, with roommates, I was always able to ask if they could please at least keep the common areas clean. With the three kids I'd just moved in with I was too scared to suggest they take their stuff up to their rooms or pick their dirty towels up off the floor for fear that I'd mess up our relationships.

Instead, I would freak out on Arne whenever his kids had trashed the common areas. It quickly became apparent that our marriage would suffer if I continued to feel helpless and take it out on him. We hoped that if we made "Keep common areas clean" one of our household rules, at least I would feel that I could safely tell the kids to clean up rather than stuff my annoyance and wait like a time bomb for Arne to get home so I could go off. I'm happy to report it worked.

I suddenly got to say, "Hey guys, remember we have to take our toys upstairs? House rule." And they would do it with only a small amount of grumbling.

If you set up detailed household rules with your husband, you can help give the kids boundaries and feel as if you have some say in what goes on in your house, without the kids thinking you're the bad guy. In other words, you're giving yourself the best publicity possible. To help you get started, here are the rules we came up with for our house.

House Rules

Living Together Rules

Be nice to each other.

Don't interrupt when someone else is talking.

If you need something, ask for it nicely and say thank you.

Whining is not asking for something politely.

Tell the truth.

Coming into the House Rules

Shoes must be placed inside the front-area bench so the
dog won't eat them.

All coats get hung up after you come inside; ask for help
if you need it. Make sure to close the closet door.

Backpacks and briefcases must be brought to the bedroom or office.

Homework Rules

All homework must be done and checked by an adult
before the television is turned on or games are played.

Bedroom Rules

Pick up and put away all toys and books before you go to
bed.

Put all dirty clothes in the dirty-clothes hamper.

Make bed in the morning.

When clothes are placed on your bed or on the stairs,
you must put them in your dresser.

If a bedroom door is shut, you must knock and wait to be
invited in.

TV area needs to be cleaned up before bed.

Bathroom Rules

Hang up wet towels on rack next to bathtub after bath or
shower.

Clothes must be picked up from the bathroom floor after
a bath or shower and put in your dirty-clothes hamper.

Flush toilet after you use it.

Put toilet seat down when you are done.

Rinse toothpaste out of sink after you brush your teeth.

Replace toilet paper or ask for help if you need it.

Kitchen and Dining Room Rules

Bring dishes to kitchen, put leftover food in trash, rinse
plate and put into dishwasher.

You either help make dinner or you help clean up after
dinner.

If dishwasher is full, empty it before you put in dirty dishes.

Put away placemat and wipe dining room table.

Living Room Rules

The couches are for sitting, not jumping.

No roughhousing in the living room; go to third floor
for that.

Because it is common space we all use and enjoy, toys,
books, etc., must be cleaned up after you're done
using them.

Who's Got the Power?

Stepmothers often complain that the children have too much
power. They affect the marriage. They change schedules. They
manipulate guilty dads, who stop enforcing rules because they
feel bad. And kids do have power in some houses. I know I
did. I took advantage of every guilty feeling my parents had
about the divorce to manipulate them to get what I wanted.

But kids need boundaries. They need rules to feel safe.
They need consistency and a feeling that even though a lot
has changed in their lives, there are some things that will remain the same. Dad will always put them to bed and read
them a story when they're at his (and your) house. They will
always have to brush their teeth and hair in the morning before school. If they do something bad, they'll get in trouble.

Because you are an adult living in the house, you're going
to be a role model, whether you like it or not. Some stepmoms jump right in to raising the children, and for some
women it works. Others take longer to feel comfortable taking on responsibility for the kids. But the fact that you have
kids in your household is not something you can take lightly.
You are affecting them every day with your personality, your
beliefs, your snits and good moods. And they are soaking up
everything you do like a sponge, even if they are pretending

to ignore you. Though it's easy to feel that you don't have any power, you do.

Georgianne never thought she'd be a full-time parent to her stepchildren. "It never occurred to me that kids who lived one hundred fifty miles away would suddenly be living with me, at least not so quickly. I did see it out there as a possibility in the future, but within six months of the marriage I was a full-time stepmom."

In Georgianne's case, she left the primary disciplining to her husband, unless she was home alone with her stepchildren. "If I didn't try to be a parent when they're alone with me, they would have run right over me." The three years she did spend with two of her four stepchildren, she put limits on the time they could spend on the phone. She demanded they do their homework before they turned on the television. She taught them how to eat properly.

Cosette, the marriage therapist, has been a stepmom of three for the past twenty years. "Stay the adult," she advises. "Have compassion and work at maintaining that you are worthy of respect and that you respect your stepchildren. And make sure you have a husband who is supportive of you and of how you deal with the kids."

If your husband supports you in front of the children and demands that they treat you with respect, then you're instantly promoted in the eyes of the kids. If they know that they can't play you against each other or sass you without getting in trouble with Dad, you stand on higher ground.

Mary, the nurse and stepmother of five who waited to marry their father until they were nearly all out of the house, agrees that a husband's support is crucial when you are relating to his children. "When I would discipline the kids, my husband would say, 'You have to listen to Mary because she's an adult. This is how you respect adults.'"

Manage Your Workload

Many stepmothers report they end up doing chores without much thought or discussion around it, as though some internalized gender role has suddenly awakened within them. And even though they are modern women with high-powered jobs, they find they expect themselves to run the house. But just because you're a woman doesn't mean that you have to do all the chores by yourself.

"I jumped into the role I thought I should fill," Mary says. She talks about the first year of her marriage: "I would come home early from work and make dinner almost every day and I'd do most of the laundry, but then I kind of lost it. I went on strike. I don't even like cooking." Eventually she and her husband negotiated that they would trade off nights to cook, and the kids, who were in high school, would do their own laundry. "I was a little over the top when I first moved in," Mary admits. "I would just go crazy. I was used to having a nice neat house, so I would have my meltdowns and the kids just got used to it."

"If you're a control freak or a neatnik, forget about it; don't do it. You have to let it go," warns Georgianne. "You have to let it go or resign yourself to being miserable all the time."

The first summer I lived full-time with my stepchildren, my stepmother sent me a check with a note that read, "Hire someone to help you with the house. It will save you." My stepmom was right. Hiring someone to help clean was the best gift I could ever have received. Now I give that gift to myself every summer when my stepkids move in.

When you start doing chores for people whom you don't feel close to yet, it can feel pretty rotten, especially if they don't treat you very nicely or if they sit on the couch and watch television while you pick up after them.

"I think one of the things that can happen is stepmothers can take on a martyr complex," says author and stepmother Anne O'Connor. "They are doing the work and nurturing because they still have the woman's role, so they think, 'Of course I'll take care of that.' Women need to be really conscious of not doing that to themselves."

The division of labor is important so you don't feel as if you're turning into the family maid. Heidi felt as if she was raising her four stepchildren since she was home with them all day, but she didn't have equal say in the bigger decisions about their welfare. "There were times I felt totally taken advantage of and not appreciated and not understood and resentful. Luckily, I do not suffer in silence."

With the help of a therapist familiar with stepfamily dynamics, she and her husband worked out a system. Even though she doesn't have the final say, she at least feels her opinion counts. "I still don't feel like I have the same authority or have the same footing that he has, but he asks my advice and consults with me about the big important things."

Really, if anyone is going to have a bit more of the workload, it's Dad. He is, after all, the one who made the decision to have children. And so, he must take responsibility for them. In our house, my husband parents his children. He gets them ready for bed and makes sure they brush their teeth. I say good night to them and read them bedtime stories with their dad when they're all ready. If their rooms are messy, I might say something like, "Wow, guys, this is a mess!" But Dad is the one that says, "Clean it up." Then I always compliment them on a cleaning job well done. You'll notice: I don't clean it for them.

Getting It Wrong

If your stepchildren are young and in your house at least 50 percent of the time, you're going to be parenting them whether you or anyone in your family acknowledges it or not. You'll be influencing how they do things when they grow up just by living in the same space. So, if you don't feel that you're part of the parenting equation because your spouse won't let you or because the kids have responded negatively to any attempts, keep in mind that you're modeling a way of living for them every moment you spend with them. Even if your stepkids are older, you're going to influence them. I was not open to any kind of parenting from my stepmother in the early days. But today, I trifold my towels just as she taught me.

Some stepmothers aren't comfortable being a parent figure because it's scary. You're going to screw up sometimes even if you read a million parenting books. So just accept that and get over it now. Kids are resilient and you'll have another opportunity to do better the next time.

I've failed many times that I know about, and probably even more times I'm not aware of, but I am forgiven every morning as a new day begins—so far. But my stepkids are not teens yet. One time I completely messed up because I didn't know what to do. It was before I considered myself a member of the parenting team. When my stepson was 8, I went to his room to tuck him in one night because it's what you're supposed to do, and he'd asked for it before. But I was still so new at it that I felt as if I was playing house, faking it. He'd been moody all day, and when I entered his room with the little-boy toys all over, he was lying in bed with a book in front of his face.

"Hey, buddy, you all ready for bed?" I asked. He wouldn't look at me. Wouldn't talk to me. His face was hidden behind the pages.

"Did you have fun today at the park?" I continued. But he still didn't answer. Finally, I read the cover of the book he was holding up. *Dinosaurs Divorce*. Instantly, I felt my body flush with old memories of my own parents' divorce, pain long since healed over. I wondered if I had become the target for his sadness at his parents' breakup. I couldn't bring myself to reach over and move the book aside. I didn't reach out and stroke his little shoulder and ask him if he wanted to talk. Instead, I bolted. I said good night as I dodged trucks and teddy bears on the floor. I fled without looking back.

I called my stepmother to ask for her advice. She was 30

when she and my father were married and she became an instant part-time stepmom.

"Don't take it personally," she said. "That was my biggest mistake."

I understood what she meant. In order to care for my stepchildren, I had to get past my own ego and try to see the world through their eyes. I had to understand that I am threatening not because of who I am but because of what I stand for in their eyes. It's impersonal. It's symbolic.

As Allison struggled through the first seven years with her stepchildren, she worked hard to be consistent. "I had to be the adult and remember that sometimes their reactions are coming through a huge filter of hurt. I couldn't be tied to the outcome. I went at them consistently with kindness and no attachment to their reaction, and eventually they came around. But I couldn't give up. You can't give up."

And don't forget all of the wonderful things about children. Their imaginations. Their exuberance and energy. You get to be a part of their future, so what kind of impact do you want to have?

DISCUSSION TOPICS FOR TWO

1. What are our house rules?
2. What are the consequences for not following the rules? How are they enforced?

3. What are our secret signals to each other so we don't argue in front of the kids?

4. How will we help support each other in front of the children?

5. Where can we each carve out personal space?

6. If we're arguing about the same things without resolution, what are some creative solutions that will make our house livable for everyone? For instance, if you're doing all the laundry and getting mad about it, can you have a laundry clinic to teach all the kids how to do their own laundry? If your stepchild knocks on the door every night and wants to sleep with you, can your husband get up and put the child back in bed and spend a few minutes calming him?

7. What is our transition plan? Kids always act up the day they move from one house to the other, so how can we make it easier on everyone?

CHAPTER 6

• •

Show Me the Money

Financial Realities

CAREER GIRL'S PERSONAL ASSISTANT

1. **Examine current status.** How much money does your household have coming in? How much do you need? How much do you want?

2. **Brainstorm possibilities.** If you're short on cash, can you come up with creative ways to make more money or spend less?

3. **Plan for expenses.** If you know your stepson needs braces in three years, start saving now. What big expenses do you know your husband has coming up? How can you help him (and you) prepare for them?

4. Dream big. What type of lifestyle do you and your husband want? What steps can you take to achieve it?

5. Enlist aid. Don't feel that you have to do this alone. A financial expert can help you navigate your stepfamily finances. However, make sure you find out if that person has worked with stepfamilies.

Money is a hot-button issue for stepfamilies. It's a tough topic for any couple. Add a remarriage between two adults who have already developed habits, and money gets even more complicated. Your husband has kids from a previous marriage to support. You might have one partner with more money than the other, a new baby together, grandparents who give unequally to step- and biological grandchildren, an ex-spouse who requires maintenance, college, estate planning, insurance, medical expenses ... are you exhausted yet? Plus, money is often used as a weapon between former spouses to get back at each other for past wrongs.

Because of the complexity of stepfamily finances, it's wise to get as much as you can hammered out with your spouse before you get married. The most important thing is that you and your husband learn how to solve money challenges together.

Some stepmothers who were formerly single career gals have assets and portfolios that are quite a bit larger than their husbands'. He may have had to split his assets down the middle in his divorce, after all, and he must continue to support a family, while a previously single stepmother has no such responsibilities. Other stepmoms find themselves having to support the household almost entirely because the amount Dad has to pay leaves him with little to contribute to his new family.

It's far too easy for a stepmother to use money as a bargaining tool as she becomes more and more resentful about the compromises she is asked to make. You're in a partnership now, however, and no matter how you divvy up the funds, you are both responsible for your combined financial health.

Ruth Hayden, a financial planner and author of the book *For Richer, Not Poorer: The Money Book for Couples,* says she stresses the importance of working through the difficult money conversations with your spouse as early as possible and getting your plans on paper, especially since stepfamily dynamics can be rife with conflict. "Even mature couples think that love is going to solve everything. As soon as you have an emotional problem with the marriage, it's exacerbated by the fear that you're going to lose half of everything you have. If the paperwork is in order and feels fair, then they shelve it. Now they can go on with their lives, and when an emotional issue hits, it doesn't get exacerbated by the fear. Paperwork is to manage fear," she says.

Hayden says she tells all of the couples she works with in which one or both partners were married before to talk about what the money issues were in previous marriages, and to be honest with each other about their financial status. "If they are absolutely clear and they are a partnership, they'll be fine."

Many stepmothers are shocked at how much money goes out to the other house, but they simply have to accept it. When you marry a man with children, he comes with a set of responsibilities he must meet. But sometimes no matter how prepared you are to accept the terms your husband agreed to with his ex when they signed the divorce papers, things can change.

Sally recalls bitterly that as soon as she and her husband, Abe, married, his ex-wife sued them for more child support. The new stepmother, who had just quit her job to pursue a lifelong dream as a singer, had to return to work to help support her husband's first family. Fair? No, but it's a reality.

Travis and his ex have joint custody of their children. They split expenses down the middle. For the most part, the system works pretty well; however, Travis—and by extension, his wife, Stacy—sometimes gets phone calls about large items the ex has bought for the children, and they are expected to pay half the bill. Things that happen in the other household will affect your financial standing, and to weather the surprises, it's critical that you and your spouse are solid financial partners. As Hayden says, doing your paperwork and learning how to approach your money lives as a partnership will keep you safe.

Setting Up Accounts

There are three basic ways to set up your accounts. The one-pot method is where each person puts any money they make into a shared account they both draw from according to needs. All household expenses come out of the pot, including anything related to the kids, such as child support payments, new clothes, school supplies, food, and toys.

The two-pot method is where each partner has their own separate account and expenses are paid separately. Usually one person will pay for the mortgage and utilities, for instance, and the other person might pay for the car insurance and food. The percentage of responsibility is calculated according to how much each person makes. Typically in this case, Dad pays for all of his children's expenses out of his own account, but the rest of the costs are split up according to who makes what. This system works well for Mary and her husband.

"We have separate accounts, no combined checking or credit cards, which works out fine," says Mary. "My husband is under the impression that he's the man and he should pay for everything, so he pays the mortgage and the car insurance. I pay for the groceries and Target runs. Then I pay for the health insurance. I do the health and dental for the kids. I put money into a retirement account and I like to travel, so I have paid for family vacations."

A third option is the yours, mine, and ours method. Both partners have their own accounts into which they put all the money they make. Then each person puts a certain amount in the combined household account every month to cover living expenses. Both partners have their own money they use at their own discretion.

This is how we have it set up in my household and it works well. My husband and I are both responsible for our own expenses, but we each fund the house account and pay house bills out of it. We always tell each other if we're spending money out of the house account, but neither of us wants to know down to the dime what the other is spending money on. As long as we meet the agreements we've made about funding our savings and bills, then the rest we don't worry about. If he needs to spend extra cash on the kids, he doesn't have to okay it with me, though we discuss it during budget meetings so that I'm in the loop. And if I want to go get a facial, if I can afford it plus meet my household obligations, then I don't have to okay it with him.

It doesn't matter which method you use as long as you're working together and you both feel that the distribution of funds is fair.

As a stepmother to your stepkids, you are not legally connected to them in any way. That means, for the most part, you are not required to financially support your stepchildren at all. (See more about this in the next chapter.)

You don't have to contribute anything to your stepchildren if you don't want to. Of course, you will be contributing indirectly, since even if you don't chip in to help fund the college tuition, your household will take a hit when your husband has to come up with the money. Your financial relationship with your stepkids will evolve as time goes on and you begin to feel more like a family. Remember that it takes an average of four to seven years for stepfamilies to bond.

If it takes you a while to feel comfortable about financially contributing to your stepkids' lives, don't worry about it. You'll be helping out just by helping their dad afford a house you can all live in or by paying for groceries for the house or vacations for the two of you when you don't have the kids. As I'm sure you already know, your financial reality as a stepmother is loaded with emotional baggage, and not just because your husband has a past life. You also bring certain emotional financial expectations to your marriage that you'll have to explore with your husband.

Getting to Know You

As you and your husband are negotiating how money will work in your household, here are some questions for you to consider. Discuss them openly with your husband—and then make sure to go do something fun afterward.

- **Disclosure.** If you sign a pre- or postnuptial agreement, you both have to disclose to the other exactly what you've got. You have to tell your spouse all of your assets and what kind of debt you're bringing to the table before anyone can sign anything. And each of you needs to hire your own lawyer for the document to be valid. So sit down and get real with each other. How much divorce debt is he coming to your marriage with? Will you share that with him? Will you help him pay it down? Do you consider it his responsibility?
- **Credit.** If your husband's name is still on his ex's house, it will be more difficult for him to get loans for your new house or the car you need now that the kids are getting bigger. He may rely on your help to finance bigger things for a while. How do you feel about his financial connection to his past?

- **Child support or alimony payments.** Find out exactly how much your husband has to pay the other household every month. This is something you're going to have to just accept. Kids are expensive, and even if you can live with the monthly number he tells you, there will be more on top of that number as the kids need sports equipment, cars, school books, braces, and tuition. It can be frustrating for stepmoms to think about what that money could do if they got to keep it within their house, especially if Mom spends it in a way you don't approve of. But don't even go there. It is what it is. Accept it and make your own money. If your husband pays alimony to his ex-wife, it's the agreement he made before you came along. It's his burden to shoulder.

- **Your contribution.** Consider what you're willing to contribute directly to your stepkids. It might not be much at first, but you can change your mind as your family begins to feel more solid.

- **Your partner's opinion.** What does your husband think is your responsibility? What does he think your financial role within the family is? Can you compromise?

- **Past relationships.** How were the finances handled in your husband's former household? Who balanced the checkbook? What were their arguments about money? Now, what about you and your former partnerships?

- **Money history.** Where do your beliefs about money come from? What did your parents teach you about money? How did they deal with their financial partnership?

Once you and your partner have decided on a financial arrangement, remember, you're going to have to be flexible. Things change. If you've decided that you're not going to pay for any of your stepchildren's expenses, examine your relationship with the kids. Will being too rigid mean you'll harm that budding connection? Alternatively, if you've agreed to help, how will you avoid feeling taken advantage of when the kids constantly bug you to buy them things on outings to the grocery store? How will you avoid guilty purchases?

To avoid last-minute buys when I take the kids out somewhere, I establish what I will or will not buy for them before we ever leave the house. For instance, if we're going to the bookstore, I tell them in advance they each get one book. When they plead for three, I remind them of our agreement. Then I can be sneaky and write down the other books they wanted for future birthday presents.

When You Make More Than He Does

If you're a career gal and you've had nothing to pay for but your own lifestyle, you are probably coming into your marriage with more than your husband. So on top of feeling the stress and strain that stepfamily dynamics put on money talks, you've also got a situation that reverses gender stereotypes.

Gretchen is the vice president of operations for a large marketing company. She remembers that she and her husband, Brad, both struggled coming to terms with the fact that she was making more money than he was. "I am the primary wage earner. We had to get over the fact that my role was to be more 'male,'" Gretchen says. "Part of his wages went to his ex-wife. We both had to work through it and get over it. I am going to have to pay for more because I make more money."

Still, even though she was prepared to enter into a partnership with a man who had kids, Gretchen had no idea when she married Brad that she would end up paying so much to support her stepchildren. "My husband still pays for child support, but I basically pay for all of my stepkids' necessities. At times I've felt like I wanted to pull my hair out since I had no way to gauge the depth of responsibility I was getting into, but I couldn't look at those kids and say no."

In this case, Gretchen paid for their clothes and winter coats. When they turned 16, she bought them each a car. But she admits she felt resentful that her stepkids' mother did not pay for the things her children needed with the child support money, especially after the kids ended up spending 75 percent of their time with their dad and Gretchen. Some of Gretchen and Brad's biggest fights have been about money, but eventually she decided she couldn't complain. "I couldn't be a martyr. I thought about my goals and my choices, and to be honest, having a family feel good was the most important thing for me."

In our household, I am not expected to pay for my stepchildren's expenses directly, but I end up contributing more to the household than my husband because most of his extra cash goes to his children. My extra money goes to maintain the lifestyle we want to live.

If you make more money than your husband does, sit down and figure out what your goals are. What feels fair? What kind of lifestyle do you want to live? What are you willing to contribute to raising those kids? Can you say no if buying an expensive toy or a new car for them makes you uncomfortable? How do your current financial arrangements affect your marriage?

Two for the Price of One

Supporting two households is more expensive than maintaining just one. And times can be pretty tight in Dad and Stepmom's house until the kids are grown, whether you make more money than your husband or not. It can be easy for a stepmom to feel the resentment build if she and her husband are struggling because of her husband's financial responsibility to his first family.

If this is the case, you're most likely going to have to decide what compromises you are willing to make for the greater good of your family. This is where your long-range planning and goal-setting skills can really come in handy. Sit down with your husband and figure out exactly how much it costs for you, him, and the kids to live in your house each month. Then tally up his separate expenses and yours. Figure out how long the money going out to the other house is going to affect your financial picture. Envision the life you want when you retire and how you'll finance it. Then you have three choices.

1. Your husband can work to make more money.
2. You can work to make more money.
3. You can both spend less.

Marie dealt with her husband Grant's financial obligations by practicing acceptance and maintaining her own income. "I made the decision to marry Grant knowing his financial arrangement with his ex. My husband had to meet his obligations. He had to financially support his son. So we had to calculate everything else based on that. I always made my own money, so I never had to rely on Grant's income. I still support myself."

Current and future expenses aren't the only things you might have to worry about. Splitting up a household can be an expensive endeavor, and you've got to know what kind of debt your husband is bringing into your marriage. If there was a credit line on his former home, he'll have to pay off half of it or more, depending on the arrangement he has with his ex. He might have to take out a loan to pay his ex for half the cost of their former home if he keeps it. They might split credit card debt down the middle or he may take it on in his name after a divorce. And it could take a long time (and considerable help from you) for him to get back on his feet financially.

"My husband was paying back a huge divorce debt. There were a lot of financial issues he had to clear up that we both knew were going to take years," says Allison. Of course, you may also be bringing debt into the marriage, which only makes things more stressful.

Financial planners such as Ruth Hayden have made money less mysterious and have come up with systems to help couples learn how to approach money as a team. So read a book. Go to a class. Learn how to manage your money lives.

It can be scary to talk about money, but once you do it and can put into place a plan that works for both you and your husband, you'll find it easier to get through any challenges that come your way in the future.

If you're resentful of the money that goes to your husband's children, you're going to have a major problem. They are a part of his life, and you have to realize that he has a responsibility to help them become successful adults. And now that you're a stepparent, you get to share some of that responsibility. Instead of thinking about what you don't have because it's going to finance decisions he made in his past life, why not instead think about how you're contributing to your stepchildren's well-being? Those kids need to be surrounded by healthy adults, and that includes being emotionally healthy about financial matters.

Or you could do what Mary did and not marry your man until the kids are out of the house. Then, at least, you won't have to deal with the daily expenses of raising children. Some women choose this route and it works for them, but remember: Just because the kids are out of the house doesn't mean there won't be expenses your partner may have to pay for, such as college tuitions and weddings.

Managing the Other House

Many stepmoms report that when Dad started regulating his payments by having them taken directly out of his check and electronically deposited into Mom's account every month, life was suddenly easier with the ex. One father says as soon as he started writing out a check at the beginning of every year that covered the entire year's child support payments, relations with his ex drastically improved.

When there is tension over money between households, the kids can smell it like bloodhounds, and they'll be the ones who suffer when either parent says, "Well, honey, I would love to be able to buy that, but your other parent doesn't give me enough money to support you." That's a pretty crappy thing to do to a kid, and it happens all the time. No matter how strained your discussions are about money, don't pass those feelings on to the kids.

Even if you enter the family when your stepchildren are adults, you will still have to deal with the financial issues that come from your husband's first family. Cheryl had to accept the financial arrangement her husband, David, made with his ex to whom he was married for more than twenty-five years. Though he had no child support payments because the youngest was 18 when David and Cheryl got together, he had already agreed to lifetime ex-spousal maintenance. Cheryl says that's not the part that bugs her; it's the feeling that she's number two that really bothers her.

"I've had a bit of an issue about being second. Even the legal system treats you like you don't have as much value as the first wife: 'The first wife, that's more important, your money needs to go there,' so then you and your second wife can't live nearly as well." When her husband asked her to help him remember to send his monthly checks, Cheryl refused. "That's your obligation," she told him. "That's your responsibility to remember." Many stepmoms are asked by their husbands to make sure the checks are sent to the ex, but I agree with Cheryl. Stay out of it. It's your husband's responsibility. He can have automatic payments set up if he has trouble remembering. Help him think creatively but stay out of the middle.

Another Mouth to Feed

If you and your husband add a new baby to the bunch, the impact that child has on your financial life will be fiscal as well as emotional.

Suddenly, your biological child gets more gifts from your family than your stepchildren do. You might feel more inclined to buy an outfit or a toy for your own child than you do for your stepchildren. But when all the kids live in the same house and see that kind of favoritism, it can hurt deeply and bring up old divorce wounds.

If you have a stepchild who throws a tantrum because your child got a toy and she didn't, it's not just about the toy. It could be that child feels rejected by her dad and displaced by your child. A compassionate conversation about how much your stepchild is loved and needed in your family could provide the balm needed to soothe hurt feelings.

You and your husband will also have to discuss how you plan to handle expenses related to the child you've had together. Don't be surprised if you have to renegotiate how you split up household financial duties now that you have a baby in common. It's natural that you'll both feel differently about the kids in your house and might have different expectations about where your money should go. Just be aware that a new baby will add a layer of complexity to your financial lives.

Estate Planning

Stepmoms are all over the board when it comes to estate planning. Because stepchildren are not included in inheritance laws, you have to clearly spell out where you want your money to go after you die. If you do not mention your stepchildren in the will, they do not exist in your world as far as the legal system is concerned. This is a relationship of choice. Just as you get to create what your role is as a stepmother, you get to decide what your financial role will be at the end of the day.

Tracy, the social scientist, adopted a daughter before she married Andrew, who had two boys of his own. When they began planning their wills, they decided to split their assets according to the fact that the boys would also be in their mothers' will. "It's not exactly even, but almost. The boys will also get money from their mother, but our daughter only has my husband and me, so there is a preference for her, but it's not a huge difference."

Mary dated her husband for eleven years while his five children grew up, but they didn't marry until the kids were nearly grown. She doesn't feel that she has a financial connection or responsibility to her adult stepchildren.

"I wouldn't want my money to go to my husband's kids," Mary says. "My beneficiaries are my husband, my brother and sister, and their kids. My husband talks about my nieces and nephews like they're mine, like people do when they both have kids. I don't know why I'm selfish like that. It just doesn't feel right. I still like to feel like I have my own family."

Because it's a relationship of choice, many stepmothers change their wills as the time spent in their stepfamily lengthens and their bonds with the children are set. Stacy is an amateur ballroom dancer, CEO of a publicity agency, and stepmom of two girls. She says she has assets amounting to several million dollars that currently will go to her husband, Travis, and her siblings in the event of her death. At this time, her stepchildren are not mentioned in her will because she and her husband have been married only a year. She plans to add them once she and Travis have been together for ten years. She also plans to reassess her will from time to time to make sure it's fair. Her biggest concern is that if she has any biological children with her husband, she would want that baby to feel as if it had siblings. "Money has a way of coming between people," Stacy says. "I wouldn't want my child to be segregated from the older children because of money."

Stephanie, on the other hand, changed her will to exclude her stepson after they could not develop a positive relationship. The rebellious teenager did everything he could to disrupt the household, especially when Stephanie and her husband, Luke, tried to set up boundaries for him. Stephanie's stepson stole things from both his father and his stepmother. He broke curfew constantly, and on one occasion was brought home by the police after a night out drinking when he was 15.

"At first my stepson was included in my will: everything just went directly to my husband and then it would go to his son. But after my bad experience with my stepson, I changed my will, and now all of my money will go to my sister. I decided my sister could use it better than my stepson, who is going to have plenty of money from his mother and father."

What you do with your money is your choice. Whatever decision you make, consider the impact of your decision on your family members and talk about it with them.

DISCUSSION TOPICS FOR TWO

1. How do we think a stepmother should contribute financially to her stepchildren? What is appropriate? In some cases, the biological mother could be upset if Stepmom provides money to stepchildren.
2. What are the financial arrangements and overall atmosphere between our home and the kids' other house?
3. What are the ways our financial life can feel fair to both of us?
4. How do we build our family's assets when part of our income goes to support another household?
5. What are our financial priorities? What makes us feel safe? Savings? Education? Owning our own home?
6. What are our short- and long-term financial goals? Paying off divorce debt? Retirement? Buying a vacation home?

7. What do we want to save for the children? College tuition? First car? Down payment on a first home? Does money from both of you go toward the kids, or just Dad's money?

8. What are you willing to contribute to your stepchildren?

CHAPTER 7

· ·

Rocky Road

The Legal Battleground

CAREER GIRL'S PERSONAL ASSISTANT

1. **Do your homework.** What do you know about the stepfamily laws in your state? What implications do they have on your life?

2. **Consult an expert.** Even if you don't intend to sign a pre- or postnuptial agreement, do you know what all the financial ramifications are for your decision to marry your partner?

3. **Review the alternatives.** Though it's no fun, consider every possible outcome. What will you do if your spouse passes away before you? What about divorce?

4. **Negotiate a deal.** Have you and your husband finished your estate planning?
5. **Assess comfort factor.** How are you feeling about
   the agreements you and your partner have arrived
   at? Are you comfortable with your financial and legal
   arrangements? If not, can you come up with a compromise?

There are few arenas in American life that can so aptly
demonstrate how ugly human beings can be to one another
as the courtroom. From divorce proceedings to custody battles to inheritance squabbles, the courtroom sees us at our
worst.

As a new stepmother, you are entering into a legal relationship with your husband that should be approached with
all the caution and preparation you'd bring to any contract.
If you're a business owner, you don't sign anything before
you know exactly what the implications of your signature
are. If you're an executive, you read that noncompete contract. If you're a contractor, you read that nondisclosure
agreement word for word before you sign. Don't you? The
same should apply to finding out the legal ramifications of
signing a marriage contract, which legally binds you and
your husband.

Use this chapter as a primer, but please consult a lawyer
familiar with stepfamily law. Since laws change all the time,
you'll have to do a little homework to make sure you know the
up-to-date information in your state.

Your Legal Relationship
with Your Stepchildren

Let's get one thing clear. You do not have a legal relationship with your stepchildren. Even though you are married to their father, you have no legal rights to those kids. In the eyes of the law, you're not related in any way. In some states, as I'll discuss later on, even though you have no legal rights, you are obligated to pay for the children living in your house, but as you'll see, your lack of legal standing regarding the kids has some pretty big implications. For instance, you are not allowed access to school records, and if your stepchild has to be rushed to the hospital, you can't give the doctors the okay to give your stepchild the care he needs. You also can't bring your stepchild to get her first driver's license because your signature isn't valid. It's a good idea to have your husband and his ex sign a legal guardianship document so that you can at least pick a stepchild up from school and take him to the hospital if there is an accident.

At this point, the laws are determined by the state you live in, and they have come into existence one at a time as issues arose. The fact that we have no legal protection or standing is a major slam for our confidence in creating a new family. So what to do? First, find out what this means for your specific family situation. Second, make sure your papers are in order—prenuptial, postnuptial, will, legal guardianship, life insurance—and are prepared by a lawyer who knows stepfamily law.

Margorie Engel has done extensive work with stepfamilies on the issues of law and finances. "Most lawyers do not seem to truly understand there is a major difference between first families and stepfamilies. A lot of damage is being done to stepfamilies. I was horrified at what kind of advice financial advisers who didn't know what they were talking about were giving stepfamilies. They were designing wills and trusts based on first-family dynamics. They weren't even asking the right questions." For more information, visit the National Stepfamily Resource Center website at www.stepfamilies.info.

Get Real

You and your husband need to disclose everything to each other. As you're creating this new partnership, you can't hold anything back. That means your husband needs to show you the divorce agreement he signed with his ex. When I first asked my husband-to-be if I could read the divorce agreement, he was reluctant to let me see it. Eventually he admitted that he was uncomfortable not because he didn't want me to know what was in it but because it felt too much as if his past life and his current life were getting too close to each other. He wanted to put as much distance between himself and his past as he could. Intellectually, he could understand why I would need to see the document. Emotionally, it was tough on him.

That's another reason the legal issues are so difficult—it's not just "A owes B this amount to care for C." All the legal arrangements are wrapped in thick bands of emotion. So practice, practice, practice discussing legal and financial issues with your husband as calmly as possible. If you have to get up and leave the room fifteen times the first night you have this discussion in order to remain cool, then do it. Even if you need to table the discussion until another night, make sure you keep coming back.

The divorce decree includes custody or visitation arrangements and explains what he has agreed to pay in child support and, in some cases, alimony to support the ex. In some divorces, he has agreed to set aside money for his children, and sometimes the ex in the event of his death, such as his insurance policy or retirement account. As someone now legally bound to the man who signed that agreement, you're going to need to know the obligations he took on before you came along.

The Other House

It's not uncommon for new stepmothers to be involved in legal battles between households during their first year of marriage—battles regarding requests for more child support and fights over custody or visitation. Sometimes this happens because a couple doesn't wait long enough to marry and Dad is still working out postdivorce arrangements with his ex. If your man is in this position, consider postponing the wedding until everything is worked out. It will make your life easier. Sometimes, no matter how long ago they worked out their agreements, an ex will decide to take a man back to court. Talk about upping the stress-o-meter.

Sometimes, however, legal battles can have a bonding effect on a man and his new wife if they feel that they've been in the trenches together and have come out stronger. That's what happened to Sue, a manager at an electronics retailer, and her husband, Matt. Sue was in graduate school for her M.B.A. when she met Matt, who was divorced and had two young children, a boy and a girl. The couple dated for five years before they married. Sue remembers the ugly custody battle with her husband's ex-wife after the ex moved to another state with their two kids and a boyfriend who was abusing the children.

"We do look back and say, 'Look at what we made it through together,'" she says. "There's a lot about the legal world that is not fair. If you think the court system is going to resolve issues, it's a mistake. It's too slow, too impersonal, too overworked. There's no way they'll get a true picture of what's going on."

The children stayed with their mother until they were old enough to say for themselves that they wanted to live with Sue and Matt. Prior to that, they were able to see the children every month even though they lived far away.

The child support payment fights had the same bonding effect on Tracy and Andrew. Three months after the couple married, Andrew lost his job and could no longer afford the high payments. He went back to court with his ex battling over custody and child support. "There was a lot of ugliness that I didn't anticipate. Suddenly this person, this ex, who up until that point had been really peripheral, was running into my life and causing all hell to break loose. One thing we learned from that year was that we are both able to handle an immense amount of stress together."

The entire first year of psychologist Sarah's marriage to her husband was lost in a fog of sadness for Sarah while her husband was wrapped up in a bitter custody battle with his ex for their two children. At first, Sarah says, she fought the good fight alongside her husband. But eventually she realized their new marriage was virtually neglected because her husband was so fueled by his anger at the ex that he could hardly concentrate on anything else. One night when he got home from work, Sarah was on the couch crying. She told him she couldn't take it anymore. When her husband finally saw what his actions were doing to his second marriage, he called up his ex that very night and they worked out an agreement over the phone in about ten minutes.

In Sally's first year of marriage to Abe, who had four children, his ex sued for more child support because she figured now that Abe was remarried, he would be able to pay more money. The courts demanded he increase his support payments, and the stepmother had to support her husband who was paying so much to the ex that he could barely contribute to their lives together.

In most states, a stepparent is not obligated to pay for the support of stepchildren. And in fact, some stepparents whose marriages end in divorce have been awarded settlements for the money they spent on stepchildren during the course of the marriage. According to Margorie Engel, however, some states obligate you to financially support your stepchildren if they live in your household. State laws often change, so make sure to find out your legal financial obligation to your step-children where you live.

Usually, however, a stepmother's financial involvement in the lives of her stepchildren is completely voluntary. So in some states, when a parent tries to sue for more child support money because a spouse has remarried and has a new stan-dard of living, the court will not award money because the child support is based on the standard of living the children had during the first marriage. However, because every judge, every court, and every state does it differently, there have been cases—as some stepmoms have discovered—in which the stepmother is not ordered to pay, but because the father's financial situation is perceived to have changed for the better owing to her income, the court demands that he pay more, even if he's not making any more money than he did at the time of the divorce.

One of the realities you must face as a stepmother is that even though you have no legal relationship with your stepchil-dren, you will still be paying for them—even if you don't buy them school clothes or pay for lessons or sports equipment. An example from our household is vacations. I love to travel. I consider travel a major priority in my life and always have. And because I am a professional woman with money of my own, I have been able to afford to travel. Now I am married to a man with kids to support, but I still want to travel. My husband can't afford to go on vacations as I can. So instead of staying home, I have offered to pay for our vacations. No, I don't pay for the kids' expenses directly (other than groceries and toilet paper, which adds up), but at the end of the day,

I'm paying for the kids, too, because my husband is. We're a team. Even though I'm not legally responsible for paying for my stepchildren, I pay. This is going to sound harsh, but kids are expensive. It's simply the reality of the situation. If I was uncomfortable with that, I shouldn't have married a man with kids.

When all is said and done, it is the biological parents who must shoulder the financial responsibility of their children in the eyes of the law, but be aware that since you're a stepmother the children will affect your financial standing as well.

Prenuptial Agreements

The last thing most people want to talk about before getting married is what they'll do if they get divorced. However, even if you ultimately decide not to sign a prenuptial agreement, the conversation you need to have in order to make one is an important step for couples and can bring you closer together.

A prenup is a document that outlines a financial agreement between you and your spouse-to-be so that in the event of divorce, your state laws and the court system are not going to make the decisions for you. For instance, if one of you has funds you've amassed before the marriage, you can protect them so they stay with you if you divorce, rather than getting divvied up as part of the marital assets. If one of you has children from a previous union and you want to designate certain funds for a college education, you can do that in a prenup.

You can even put in things such as how you will pay bills and how you will handle credit card debt. Certain things are not covered under a prenup, such as property division if you divorce, custody of children, and child and ex-spousal support.

It is certainly a smart thing to do if you've got a company or earn a substantially larger amount than your spouse. However, a prenup is also an emotional decision. Some stepmothers decide not to sign one because they feel it's sending their husbands the message that they aren't totally committed to the marriage, since they're already planning for divorce.

Others say they would recommend signing one because it's "just being realistic." Heads up though: Prenups don't always stand up in court. If one spouse has a lot of money, for instance, and another one will leave the marriage practically destitute, a judge may rule the prenup null and void and award a 50–50 split anyway. If you're not married but are living together, you can draw up a cohabitation agreement, which covers the same items as a prenup.

Postnuptial Agreements

A postnuptial agreement, also called a marital contract, is a document signed after your marriage. In the contract, you can address property division in the case of divorce. This agreement can also outline financial agreements you'll adhere to if you remain married, such as how you will pay for long-term care if one or both of you need it during your retirement years or in case of an accident or illness.

Wills

We've all heard it: The earlier you execute your will, the better. And in a stepfamily, it's even more important if you want your money to go where you say it should go. As I mentioned earlier, stepchildren are not included in inheritance laws. So if you die without naming them in your will, they get zip, and even if you do name them, a court could award your money to a blood relative if the wording of your will is vague in any way. If you consider your stepchildren family and want to provide for them when you're gone, then you've got to make sure your will is airtight. The more money you have, the more important it's going to be.

That means finding a lawyer who is familiar with stepfamily law. Hopefully, no one will contest your will, but you never know how your family members will react after you're gone. It can get nasty for stepchildren, so take the burden off them and your husband and get that will put together.

If you have a child together and you and your husband die without a will, your stepchildren could be out in the cold no matter what you intended to give them, and all of your assets would pass to your biological child, no matter how long you lived with your stepchildren, even if they lived with you full-time since they were babies and their mother has never been in the picture.

Talk with your lawyer about the house or any other property you own, insurance policies, retirement accounts, investments, cash, and any personal items you want to name for specific family members. You might want to set up a trust so there will be no questions about where you want your money to go. You'll also want to include how your debt will be paid in the event that you die with debt.

Many stepmothers are uncomfortable naming their step-children in their wills right away and wait until they've been a part of the family for a decade or more before they change their wills to reflect the closeness of the relationship. Other women decide to put the stepkids in right away. And some stepmoms leave money equally to their stepchildren and bio-logical children because they don't want to drive a wedge be-tween the siblings.

Make sure your husband's will is in order, too, and that you know what it says. If your husband dies before you do, you'll want to make sure you are taken care of and the children are also considered. You don't want to be a stepmom who dukes it out with her stepkids once Dad is gone over what he's done in his will. In fact, it's better if you sit down with all of the kids before anyone goes anywhere and let them know what you plan to do with your estates so there are no surprises at a time when everyone will be grieving.

Darcy is a human resources manager who became a step-mother of two children. After she and her husband married, they had two kids together. "If we both die, we have a living trust so that all four of the kids receive equal amounts," Darcy says. "In the event that my husband dies first, I would take what I need to live on and then split the excess four ways."

Judy, a counselor and management consultant, doesn't have kids of her own. She's left everything to her stepchildren. "I don't know if they would have gotten everything if my siblings' kids were in need, but every one of my siblings is better off than I am, so it hasn't been an issue."

Mary, the nurse who waited eleven years to marry Pat, wants her nieces and nephews to inherit her assets. She figures her five stepchildren have plenty of money coming from their mother's family and from their father.

Plan for Your Golden Years

As you and your husband plan your retirement years, make sure you address issues such as what happens if he dies before you and his kids have to choose your care facility in your old age, or pay for it. Make sure to plan so that you will not be left out on the street by resentful stepkids.

Gretchen has worried about her elderly years, even though her relationship with her two stepchildren is strong. "My own insecurity has been that if anything happens to my husband, then I'll be alone—even though the kids have been very candid about saying to me, 'If you guys ever get divorced, we would want you to have custody.'"

Ending up alone is a fear that a lot of stepmothers have, and rightly so. What guarantee do we have that our stepchildren will visit us and care for us when we need it? Gretchen has put away much of her salary, so she knows she's financially safe. Like Gretchen, plan to have enough for your retirement years—and continue developing those relationships with the kids.

Children in stepfamilies that stick together for decades

often feel they have two nuclear families, or a binuclear family, once the early upheaval is over and everyone has settled into feeling like family. I definitely have two nuclear families, and I feel responsible for knowing what's going to happen to the parents and stepparents on both sides as they enter their seventies, eighties, and nineties. It's my job as a child of both houses to make sure that no one is left out on the street. I know they have all set up plans for themselves, but if it came down to it, I would make sure they're covered. It's what families do.

At this point I don't expect that kind of dedication from my stepchildren. It's still too early. I wish to develop the kind of relationships with them that stand the tests of time. If something happened to their father, I hope they would still feel a connection to me.

Adoption

There is a way for a stepfamily to be considered equal to a first family in the eyes of the legal system. If you adopt your stepchildren, then all the rights of the noncustodial parent are severed, and you and your stepchildren gain all of the rights afforded to parents and their kids. However, though adoption by stepparents is on the rise, it's still a difficult thing to do if the other biological parent is still living.

First, you and your husband have to get buy-in from the kids. The older they are, the more say they have in the eyes of the law. Second, the biological mother has to sign away all her rights to the child or you have to prove beyond a doubt that she is an unfit mother. Because it's very hard to prove a mother is unfit to parent her children and it's a permanent decision, stepmothers usually don't attempt adoption unless it's an extreme case—if Mom is an incarcerated drug addict or severely abusive, for instance.

When Mom is deceased, you can legally adopt stepchildren as long as Dad and the children find it acceptable.

If You Divorce

I will mention this only briefly because I'm sure everyone reading this book is going to make it! But in the case of a divorce, a stepparent's obligations to the stepchild stop immediately, except for a few rare cases in which some stepparents are ordered to pay child support. You had no legal relationship with them to begin with, and you have even less of a reason to be connected with them if you divorce their father.

There is a legal term, *in loco parentis*, which means "in the place of a parent." If you have acted as a parent to your stepchildren from a very young age and for a long period of time, you may be able to get visitation or even custody rights if you can prove that the child has an emotional bond to you. But even a strong long-term bond doesn't necessarily mean a court will rule in your favor. Biological parents win most of the time, even if it would be good for the kids to get to see you.

Get It Done

It's worth repeating: Do your homework and your paperwork. Otherwise your family could be left with a mess when you die, and that's just not nice to do to them.

DISCUSSION TOPICS FOR TWO

1. How do we want to provide for our family when we're gone?
2. What happens if one of us dies before the other?
3. If we're in the middle of a legal battle, how can we creatively settle our differences with the other household in a way that's best for the children?
4. What paperwork do we need to get in order?
5. Do we need a prenup or postnup agreement?
6. Can we get a legal guardianship document for Stepmom signed by Mom?
7. In the event of a legal confrontation with Dad's ex, what can we do to maintain positive feelings in our marriage? What ways can we relieve stress?
8. Are we each open to working with a lawyer knowledgeable of stepfamily issues to help us do our wills? Soon?

CHAPTER 8

You're the Boss (of Yourself)

Empowered, Educated Women Make Good Stepmoms

CAREER GIRL'S PERSONAL ASSISTANT

1. **Find your power sources.** What things inspire you? What makes you feel strong and confident?

2. **Create an action plan.** In those moments when you feel powerless or voiceless, what will you do? How will you express yourself? How will you give yourself a voice?

3. **Get educated.** Are you willing to accept that yours is not a first family and learn what makes stepfamilies successful? How about your husband and the kids? Are they willing?

4. Team-build. What rituals can you establish that will help your stepfamily bond? Building a playhouse? Camping?
5. Protect downtime. We all need breaks. How will you get yours?

When you decide to marry a man with children, your life-style will change, but that doesn't mean giving up your power and becoming invisible. You are the adult, and you have power. You have the ability to make decisions and carry them out. To become an empowered stepmother, you have to understand and find peace with the fact that you will always be a bit of an outsider.

Jessica, who now has a close relationship with her step-mother, still doesn't consider her part of her inner circle. "Family is not perfect. It's an art, not a science. I've lived it for a long time; every time there is a wedding or graduation we live through it all over again. I think it's hard on the step-parents. The more stepparents want to do the job well, the harder it's going to be on them. My stepmother has been in my life for twenty-five years, but when I think about my nu-clear family, that picture has never changed. It's my parents, and then my stepparents are in the outer sphere."

This is the reality. You're never going to be a mother to your stepchildren. They may like you and grow to love you and include you when they talk about their families, but your role in the family is one that you need to create for yourself. You need to figure out how to feel empowered because power affects every relationship within a stepfamily. The slow-drip water torture of daily reminders that you are a bit outside the family unit—the innocent reference to things that happened before you came along, for instance—can erode your power. Get used to those small reminders because they don't go away.

A powerless stepmom can feel as if everyone is out to take her husband's time, money, and attention away from her. But you can learn to negotiate stepfamily dynamics as well as you do office politics.

One of the best techniques to start with is one recommended by Cherie Burns in her book *Stepmotherhood*. She asserts that children are used to having adults tell them what to do. She suggests taking on more of a teacher or coach role. That way you can maintain some emotional distance and still feel okay about setting boundaries within your household.

For instance, when I first began integrating with my new stepfamily, I was so emotionally overwhelmed that I took every single thing the kids did personally. (I still do, sometimes.) It's a common and ongoing reaction for stepmothers that outsiders simply cannot understand unless they live in a stepfamily themselves.

Even though I am a mature professional woman, I would unravel at the dinner table when my stepkids would talk with their mouths full. At first I assumed they were doing it on purpose to annoy me. Instead of simply telling them not to talk with their mouths full, as any sane and rational human being would do, I would sit and fume and keep my mouth shut so that by the time I left the table, I was completely enraged.

Finally I decided to try the coach-teacher route to see if it would help. Before we sat down to dinner, I would imagine that I was a teacher entering a classroom. When any of my stepchildren opened their mouths with bits and pieces of the dinner I made hanging out, I said, "Honey, we don't eat like that at the table. Chew with your mouth closed, please. Then you can talk." Like a teacher explaining how to multiply 7 times 7, I wasn't emotionally invested. My stepchildren could sense that and immediately responded. They closed their mouths and chewed their food, then told us about their day at school. I've used the technique many times since with positive results.

Education

I was at a dinner party recently where I met a woman who, as it turned out, also has three stepchildren. Her eyes lit up when she discovered I was working on this book, and she started asking me all sorts of questions. She said she'd been married for two and a half years, and when she first moved in with her husband and the kids, she had looked for information to help her but hadn't been able to find anything. She said that when she got involved with her husband, she didn't know any divorced families and had absolutely no clue about what to expect.

I've heard that story more times than I can count.

If you know how stepfamily development operates, wouldn't you feel better equipped to handle the common blowups as they come along? If you knew that it's completely normal for children to start acting horrible to you the more they like you because it makes them feel disloyal to their mother, wouldn't that help you address it in a way that eased the burden on the kids and changed the behavior?

Before I read a single word about stepfamilies, I remember sitting down to dinners with my stepkids on their first night back from staying at their mom's house. Every single Friday they were bears. They were always loud and unruly, and usually a fight broke out between the siblings. I knew they were acting out because of the transition of moving from one house to the other. I'd lived it myself as a child. I can't imagine what a stepmom who had no knowledge of stepfamilies at all would think in those moments.

I, too, go through the transition of having them reenter our lives every weekend. I have to adjust from time alone with their dad to time with the whole stepfamily. I discovered that it was better if I also had some alone time. Because I know how these transitions affect the kids and me, I feel empowered. I feel that I can manage the amount of chaos in the house because I know what is driving it.

Here's another example. I've known my youngest stepdaughter since she was 3 years old, and she and I have a close bond. We enjoy each other's company quite a lot. One day her father was playing around, being silly, and I jokingly said to him, "Stop that or you're grounded." Immediately my stepdaughter leaped to her father's defense. She told me if I grounded her dad, she would ground me.

I was hurt because her response was a reminder of my

outsider status. Then I got angry because no one is allowed to be in the middle of my relationship with my husband. And then the voice of reason clicked on in my head. I knew what my response to my stepdaughter had to be. I had to joke around with her and call her a "Daddy's girl," and say how lucky her father was to have such a wonderful daughter who would come to his rescue. Because that is my job as a stepmother. I know that when a stepmother gets into a contest with a kid over the child's dad, there is no winner. I knew I had to be the adult and keep my emotions in check.

In stepfamilies, when emotionally loaded things like this happen, the family splits down biological lines. Since I don't have children of my own, I don't have my own family to comfort me, so I am left out, while my husband takes solace from the love of his children. I felt better being able to identify what was happening and why I felt so crappy about such a little thing.

"Be prepared" is as good a motto for new stepmoms as it is for the Boy Scouts. Would you attempt to get your M.B.A. or your law degree without reading any of the textbooks or attending any of the lectures? Check out the resources at the end of this book for recommendations on the very best tools for further preparing yourself for instant-family life.

Conflict Resolution

A lot of time is spent in companies across the country helping people learn conflict management skills. In marriage education classes you learn about how to negotiate and deal with conflict; as we all know, it's part of daily life with another human being. A stepfamily will really put your conflict resolution skills to the test.

- **Marital relationship.** Get a babysitter so you and your husband can go somewhere to discuss how you're going to approach the problem your household is having. You're a united front. Use the well-known "I" statements ("I feel as if ...") rather than "You" statements ("You always ..."). If things get too heated, take a break.

- **Arguing with the kids.** Most stepfamily experts will tell you not to confront your stepchildren directly until your relationship is strong enough to handle it. At first a stepmother's only way to deal with conflict is to bite her tongue and go through her husband. If Dad is not home, you get to enforce the household rules. Stay calm and use logical explanations with the kids. The conflict will escalate if you lose control of your emotions. If possible, take the child you're having difficulties with out for one-on-one time—a ride in the car, a bike ride, or a walk—so that you can talk but the child doesn't have to look you in the eye. That way it's easier for the child to open up.

- **Consider the outcome.** Think about what you want to get out of the discussion so you know before going in what you're willing to settle for. Like negotiating a salary at a new job, know what your lowest bid would be and ask for more so you have room to negotiate.

- Be calm, cool, and collected. The more peaceful you are with your stepchildren, the more you'll be able to influence them. If you find yourself spiraling into anger or tears, leave the room, collect yourself, and return to the fray after some deep breaths. First of all, you don't want the kids to know they have enough power over you to make you lose your temper, because they will take advantage of it. Second, you'll be able to make rational, proactive decisions only if you're calm.
- Let Dad handle it. Why not? That's one of the perks of being a stepmother. They're his kids. Let him deal with it. Then you aren't the bad guy. Besides, most children take discipline much better from their biological parents. Then you can continue to work on building your relationship with the kids while improving your negotiating skills with your husband at the same time.
- Have a signal. When something happens and you want to alert your husband to it, have a signal so the kids don't hear you arguing in front of them.
- Know when to say you're sorry. Since saying "I do," I have had to say "I'm sorry" more times than ever before. Part of successfully resolving conflict means being able to admit when you're off base. That is hard to do sometimes, but if you apologize to your husband and your stepchildren, you are more accessible as a human being. You're admitting that you're not perfect, and you're doing the best you can.
- Breathe and let go. All stepmothers will tell you to pick your battles. There are some things that in the

long run just aren't worth fighting over. "If you whine about every single thing, you're just a nag, but if you let the little stuff go, when you bring something up, and say, 'It hurts my feelings when ...', then you can actually get somewhere," says Sandy. There are things that will happen in your stepfamily you don't agree with. For instance, your husband and his ex may decide to send your stepchildren to a school you don't approve of. You have every right to discuss it with your partner and voice your opinion, but the final decision is theirs.

• Be creative. Practice thinking outside the box and you'll be better equipped to solve the common problems in stepfamily life. When Brad was having trouble communicating with his ex-wife, his second wife, Gretchen, experimented. Gretchen called the explosion-prone ex to see if she could manage the kids' schedule. When that didn't work, she started using the fax machine to get messages to the other house. Negotiating schedules and child expenses between the houses became much easier for Brad and Gretchen when it was done in such an impersonal way.

Mine Your Advantages

There is much power in your placement as the "intimate outsider." You have the ability to see the big picture, when sometimes a parent can't. You can be an objective eye for a dad who is having difficulty communicating with a troubled kid.

You can advise your husband on ways to keep a long-distance relationship with a child who lives far away.

When Cheryl and David met before the end of his divorce to his first wife, Cheryl knew she had to help her husband keep his relationships with his kids. "I always reminded myself of something my father said was one of his guiding principles: You always keep the communication channels open. You don't have to like what your kids do, you don't have to approve of it, but you have to keep the communication going. I helped my husband maintain that connection and relationship with his children."

I slip in little statements to my stepkids every now and then, such as, "Your father loves you so much," or "Your dad thinks you're so smart," or "I know your father loves to spend time with you." That way I can make sure they know it's important to me that they have a good and strong relationship with Arne. It makes me feel as if I am helping, which in turn makes me feel that I have some power in my house to encourage positive growth.

Another wonderful advantage of being the intimate outsider is that you get to check out when you need to, as Mary discovered. "Earplugs! There are advantages to being able to say 'They're your kids.' I am pretty sensitive to lack of sleep and make sure I get my required hours in if I can." Mary doesn't feel bad about putting boundaries around her needs. When she's well rested, she's a better wife and stepmother.

In our house, when I need to work, Arne takes full responsibility for his kids and makes sure I'm not disturbed. They play together and he makes dinner while I finish up an interview or a writing project. Then I can join them when I have finished what I need to, and can fully participate without feeling resentful that I had to sacrifice my work to take care of Arne's children. And the kids get to spend time with their dad. Since they know I'm working, they don't take my absence personally.

Allison made the most of her role by doing things with her stepchildren she liked to do. She made a list of all the things she loved, and then set herself on a mission to help the kids do things they'd never done before. "I always had a plan when the kids were with us. Something they had never thought of before. They all thought they wouldn't like sushi, but I said you have to at least expose yourself to it. Let's have fun trying new things. It can break the rigidity that happens when everyone shuts down."

The "A" Team

The single most important thing you need to make you feel empowered in your own home is the support of your husband. It's so easy for stepmothers to feel insecure in the first years of a new marriage with a man who has children, so make sure you are working on your relationship. It will give you power. Even in situations where you feel as if you have no say, it won't be as big a deal because you can be confident in your relationship with your husband. It's when you're not confident about the strength of that bond that stepfamily issues are amplified into insurmountable obstacles.

When Allison and Charles got in trouble during their first
year of marriage, they attended a marriage education course.
"As our relationship improved, my ability to become a stepmom grew. I had to stretch myself to get my brain, heart,
and ego around the many gnarly surprises that went along
with stepmotherhood. There were times when I felt like my
husband was throwing me to the wolves. But once he and I
could actually talk, the things we fought about became topics
for discussion."

Cosette believes the positive relationship she has with her
stepchildren is largely due to her husband, Paul. "My stepchildren knew they were to treat me with great respect. The
fact that my husband enforced that is huge."

In Stephanie's home, her husband's lack of power with
his son dramatically influenced the child's rotten behavior
toward his stepmother. "My husband is a good man, but he
allowed his child to treat me badly because he allowed his son
to treat him badly. The custodial parent is the key. If there is
respect there and good boundaries, there's a greater chance
for someone else to enter."

So how do you get your husband to step up to the plate,
if he hasn't already? You can suggest working with a trained
stepfamily therapist. You can read books together about stepfamilies. The National Stepfamily Resource Center at Auburn University in Alabama has all the tools you need to learn
about stepfamily life.

Have those "down to the bone" conversations, but when
you do have painful discussions about his past—or about why
he feels that he can leave the parenting of his children to you—

make sure you have a list of next steps that can help you both feel empowered. Michele Wiener-Davis is a marriage therapist and the author of *Divorce Busting*. She believes that if one person shows up in a therapist's office ready to work but the other refuses to attend, change can still happen in the relationship. "If you change your behavior toward your significant other, you will get different results," she says.

If your husband is allowing the children to treat you without respect, perhaps you need to start leaving the room if they act disrespectfully toward you. You are a human being, and it's okay to expect to be treated with civility in your own home. If your husband is not enforcing that rule, show him that it's important to you. If you consistently treat your husband and the kids with respect, you'll find that they will eventually respond to that respect.

Carve out a place in the house that is all yours and where you have complete control. If you have an office, the children must do as you say in it. Make those the rules of engagement if they want to enter. Make sure your husband is also willing to learn about stepfamily life. If he won't read a book, set up nights to tell him what you've learned from those you've read.

It's easy to lose yourself, your voice, your self-worth in an environment that tests the very strongest among us. But you do have power. You are a human being with a purpose on this earth. You deserve to be treated with care and respect even by people who are wounded. Keep your head held high, ladies. It's an uphill battle sometimes, but you get to create the role you want for yourself. So do it consciously.

DISCUSSION TOPICS FOR TWO

1. What makes you feel confident?
2. In what ways can Dad support Stepmom's role with the kids?
3. What are the advantages of being a stepmother?
4. What skills can Stepmom bring home from work and use to solidify our relationships?
5. Where can we go for help? A support group? A counselor? Family? Friends? The library?

CHAPTER 9

Pit of Despair

Fight the Instant-Family Funk

CAREER GIRL'S PERSONAL ASSISTANT

1. Hire help. What kind of help do you need? Someone to pick up the dry cleaning? A counselor to guide you through the beginning stages of stepfamily life?
2. Research yourself. What makes you happy?
3. Assess your behavior. What is your role in the chaos? Are you doing anything to fuel the discomfort in your home? Are you freaking out about things you have no control over?
4. Record your wins. What progress have you made? Are you a more mature person? Have you accepted your own

peccadilloes? Have you helped open your stepchildren's eyes to something new?

5. **Rewards for a job well done.** What will you give yourself? A facial? A weekend away with your girl-friends? A new outfit?

Just scroll through one of the online chat rooms, boards, and forums for stepmothers and you'll discover to what depths of despair stepmotherhood can drive a woman. Here is a sampling of the topic headers you can find online from distraught stepmoms.

Left out
Should I stay or should I go?
What a mess!
Worried all the time
Fed up! Why do I bother?
Hating husband's ex
It's not fair!
Lost everything
Is there a light at the end of the tunnel?
Am I crazy?
When will home feel like home again?

The tensions within a stepfamily have deep roots, and step-mothers with no experience often feel lost. It's quite common for stepmothers to cast themselves in the role of martyr. When I talked to stepfamily experts while researching this book, one of the comments I heard most often was this: "Please tell me your book is not a 'woe is me' book for stepmothers." If you read through the comments posted on the chat boards, it certainly does sound as if there's a big pity party going on. For so many stepmothers trapped in a home in which they feel that they have no power, it's easy to take on the role of the victim.

I acknowledge that being a stepmother is difficult. I have locked myself in the bathroom and cried. I have felt like an idiot because I didn't know what I was doing. I've felt that I have no say in what goes on in my own home. But I can't just leave it at that. I need to do something about it. Imagine spending your life living at the mercy of your stepchildren or your husband's ex-wife. No thanks.

The only way out of the pit of despair is to take action.

Strategies to Help You Get Off the Couch

When you're stressed, what do you do to make yourself feel better? And, no, yelling at your husband is not an effective means of releasing stress. It may make you feel better in the moment, but eroding your marital relationship is not the way to go. Here are some suggestions to help you in your darkest moments when your home feels like a battleground.

Team Building

You're a talented woman. So why not remember the skills you have in your working world and use them at home? When you've got a problem at work, think about how you find a solution. Do you get things done when you take everything personally and attack your coworkers or employees? No. Do you create a harmonious and success-oriented environment when you demand that everyone keep their desks exactly the way you want them? No.

How *do* you promote teamwork?

You find out what everyone's strengths are. You help everyone feel that they have a stake in the company's success.

If something happens at work, how do you regroup and gather energy for the next project? How do you fire yourself back up and get excited about the job ahead? Can you do that for yourself in your home life? Can you build a team at home in which everyone feels they are an integral part of the forward motion of the family? Can you build something that gives every member personal satisfaction because they feel that they have some say about the direction of the family?

Many stepfamilies use weekly or monthly family meetings to check in with one another. Gretchen and her family held family meeting nights to discuss personal or household issues. Then one member of the group would get to pick what they had for dinner and a fun activity to do together as a family after the meeting was over. It became a great way to build camaraderie for this stepfamily, because they ended up enjoying one another's company while creating traditions.

Retreat, Restore, Return

My husband and I have a tradition that has proven to be very valuable to our marriage. Every time one of us is out of town, we write each other letters. During the early days of new stepmotherhood, when I was overwhelmed with work, the move, the kids, the husband, I decided to get away for a few days by myself to our family cabin. So I wrote him a letter. I explored the reasons I was feeling so stressed out and then wrote about all the reasons I had decided to marry him. I wrote all of the things I like about my stepkids and what I thought I had learned from them so far.

By the time I got home two days later, my funk had lifted and I was able to get back in the game. If you don't have a cabin or some other space you can retreat to, you can rent one or get a hotel room somewhere in a cute little town. Bed-and-breakfasts can also be a fun option. If these aren't in the budget, perhaps a friend would let you borrow her house or apartment for a few days while she's away, in exchange for walking her dogs or watering her plants. The key is to learn what you need to replenish yourself, and then set the boundaries around it so you don't have to reach the bottom of your well before you do something to recharge your battery.

Running Errands

Sometimes just getting out of the house for a while is enough to get my mood back on track. If I need a break from the chaos, I take the shopping list and head out for an afternoon on my own. I get to cool off with a break between errands at a coffee shop or lunch spot, while Arne gets to spend quality time with his kids. Sometimes I sneak away to a movie in the middle of the day. Stepmoms often feel guilty about taking time out for themselves when the kids are around, but you'll be a better stepmom if you keep doing things for yourself.

This can backfire if you're gone all the time, however. Just like anything else, it's a balance. You don't want the kids or your husband to feel that you don't want to be around them at all.

Leave It in the Middle

When Allison became a stepmother, she found herself a target of negativity from both her stepchildren and her husband as they worked to get over old divorce wounds. "I came to realize there was a tremendous amount of anger, resentment, and confusion in the kids. All of those deep-seated, unexpressed feelings of frustration were directed at me, even with my husband. I felt like the dumping ground for everything," she says.

On the days when she couldn't stand it, she would have lunch with one or two of her girlfriends and let all of her frustrations out in conversation. "We took a timer with us. One was the timekeeper; one was the spewer. We said, here's the deal, we love life, we love our children and our husbands, but we can say whatever we need to say here and we'll leave it in the middle of the table. Because we all know we're going to drive back home, but we're glad we got it out of our system. There need to be a lot of outlets for that resentment and frustration and venom."

Let It Grow

Remember that all of this takes time to develop. Your identity as a stepmother will evolve and you'll discover what you think is important. "I had a small, narrow, selfish life," says Heidi of her days as a family law attorney before her four stepchildren entered her life. "I know my character flaws a lot more now, but I think it's better to be aware of them. I've grown a lot and I know what's important to me. I was so caught up in the status of things, of eating at the right restaurant and doing all of those things a single woman does when I could afford to. Now I can't go out all the time and spend money, but I would rather have spaghetti and meatballs with my stepkids than anything."

Take Care of Yourself

Gretchen says that years five through seven of her marriage to a man with two kids were the hardest for her. "The kids were going through their own stages, so I was dealing with the kids' evolution and work pressures, and I wasn't taking care of myself." Gretchen ran herself ragged until she realized she had to take care of herself to keep healthy. That's when she started seeing a life coach to help her develop strategies for self-care.

Mary, who married her husband, Pat, after dating for eleven years, found a way to ensure her sanity. "My saving grace has been my travels with friends. I've been to Australia, Peru, and Ireland without husband or children since I got married. I am always happy to come back, and we all appreciate each other more after my return."

Even when Debra is not training for a marathon, she runs in the morning to burn off stress and have alone time.

I take care of myself by maintaining a ritual I've performed for years. Every morning I get up early, before everyone else in the house. I make coffee and grab a book and my journal. I turn on music and read for a while, then write in my journal. Those daily peaceful moments help me keep my balance.

Reconnect with Your Husband

John Gottman believes that couples should have high expectations of their marriage. Turn your husband into your sanctuary. Tell him you need to spend time with him. If you can't find a babysitter, put the kids to bed, put on a movie, and snuggle with your husband on the couch. Or go for a walk together and hold hands. Do something you both love. Sleep in. Lie on the couch with your feet on his lap and talk about your dreams for the future. If you connect with your husband, it will make you feel that you can face anything—even his rebellious teenage son who has been kicked out of school again or threatened to burn the house down. It's the two of you against the world!

Get Physical

Exercise is a proven way to release stress and up the feel-good hormones in your body. And it's no coincidence that a large number of the stepmothers I interviewed are in the best shape of their lives. A long, I mean *really* long, walk or a trip to the gym or a personal trainer or a yoga studio are fantastic ways to destress. And you don't have to make excuses to exercise. Husbands and stepkids understand the need for exercise. It's culturally acceptable to take me-time if it's related to getting in shape.

Physical movement is an important tool for relieving tension, even if it's not actually exercise. "Sometimes I would get in the shower and I'd be full of all this toxic energy and I would shake myself from head to toe," Allison says. "The more tense you are, the more tied up in knots, the stiffer you are and you can't let things flow through you. I would start shaking so hard that sometimes I would start to cry and then I would start to laugh."

Reminders

I often use physical objects to help me remember things in the moment. For instance, I have a bracelet that reminds me every time I wear it that it's my intention to have an open heart with my stepkids. It reminds me that no matter how I am feeling in the moment, I need to remember what it's like to look at our stepfamily life through their eyes. I may feel yucky, but at least I have control over my situation. I can get in my car and drive to the mall. I can tell them to go to their rooms. I can get on a plane and go visit my friends. Those kids can't. They have no control over when they come and go from one house to the next. I wouldn't wish being a stepchild on anybody. Compared to the kids, I've got it easy.

Ego Management

When I asked what advice women would give to new stepmothers, by far the most common thought was "Don't take it personally." It's easy for your ego to get wounded when you don't feel that you belong to the "in" crowd in your stepfamily. Instead of reacting to a comment from your stepchild that you feel is directed at you, why not take a moment first and breathe? This is much harder than it sounds.

My friend Deanna is a first-grade teacher. She was taught that when dealing with a room full of 6-year-olds, you do not let your first reaction rule you. When she feels her anger flash through her when a kid says or does something out of line, she counts. My friend takes her ten seconds (sometimes she even counts out loud in front of the class) and breathes. Then she can look at the situation and try to figure out what she's going to do using all of her faculties, instead of reacting from a wounded ego.

Trying to get away from letting your ego rule you is challenging. The more you practice, the easier it gets. "You really have to work at not having your ego out there taking offense at everything," says Cosette, a twenty-year veteran stepmom. "You can't take offense. Otherwise you would be upset all the time. You can't do that."

Successfully managing your ego is also about knowing when to let things go. "If you let everything bother you, you aren't going to make it in the marriage," says Bonnie Rudden, a counselor in St. Louis, Missouri, who specializes in stepfamily issues. "Choose your battles," she advises.

It feels like a little jab to me every time the kids say "Dad's house" when they refer to our home, especially considering the amount of money I've spent on the place. Even though I want to correct them and say, "Dad *and* Jacque's house," every time they say it, I keep my mouth shut. Sometimes they do say "Dad and Jacque's house." Sometimes they say "our house." Either way, we all live together in the same house, and that's what's important.

Reach Out

Surround yourself with support. Heidi knows what she could have done that would have helped her through her early stepfamily years when she moved away from her parents, whom she'd never lived more than an hour from. "I should have reached out more to my family and friends back home, but I didn't. Part of the reason I didn't was that I felt it would be disloyal to the kids and my husband if I did."

To enlist aid is not disloyal; it's just the opposite, when you consider how close friends can help you gain perspective. If you do reach out for support, find people who can understand and empathize. A troubled stepmother who asks for support from a friend without a clue about stepfamilies can end up feeling even worse. Choose your confidants wisely.

"Education only goes so far" advises author and stepmom Anne O'Connor. "You have to have support in the form of people who will listen to you." But it can't be just anyone.

Stepmoms Like Me

There's comfort in numbers. So finding a group of stepmoms you can hang with and dish to is a huge help. But be forewarned: Stepmom groups can be overwhelmed with negativity. Find people you can confide in that help you feel hopeful.

Mary attended a stepmom education class held by psychologist Ann Orchard in Minneapolis. After the six-week session was over, her group continued to meet for support and friendship. "You can say anything, and whatever you say, you feel like you're not going to be judged. And even though every step situation is unique, they can get it."

Twelve years into her partnership with a woman who has two children, Lisa wishes she had found a group of women to talk to instead of routinely locking herself into her tiny office. "You can't tell the kids your feelings, because that's not appropriate. And you can't express it to your partner, because it only serves as fodder for a fight. I had no place to vent this stuff. So I just sucked it up and became resentful."

Try to join a group that helps you think positively and problem-solve as well as one that helps you vent your anger. Anne O'Connor cautions all the stepmoms she talks to: "It can really help if you have a group of women you meet with and all you do is sit around and mope and moan, but stay away from the sites where women are screeching and angry. That's okay as long as there's a 'Yeah, but what are you going to do about it?' You need the evolution that follows. When I tell people to go and find help, I tell them to avoid people who are pissed off and without any apparent interest to get through it. You've got to do something with that anger or it will eat you alive."

Judy, a stepmom of three for the past twenty years, agrees. She uses her skills as a counselor to develop her own strong relationships with other stepmoms. "It's critical that people come out of hiding. A stepmother is not an evil person. I am a human being and it's a hard job. I want the love and support of other women to give me perspective when the rest of the world is clueless."

Go for Help

Don't be ashamed to get help. And make sure the help you get is qualified. Many marriage and family therapists in the United States are given no training in stepfamily dynamics. With stepfamilies outnumbering nuclear families in this country, how is this possible? In a study by John and Emily Visher, 53 percent of the families polled said they did not get the help they needed from a therapist because they felt they knew more about stepfamily dynamics than their therapists. So make sure your therapist has done his or her homework.

Figure Out Your Priorities

If you're in a high-conflict situation with older stepkids who are acting out in dangerous ways, such as doing drugs, stealing, or threatening or acting out violence, you've really got to reach down deep into your reserves of inner strength, because the tension surrounding your marriage can spill over into it. In that situation, your job is to step back and let the biological parent deal with the child. Do your best to be supportive behind the scenes. Make a list of your priorities. What do you want out of this marriage? What do you want your relationship with the kids to be like? What are your deal-breakers?

Don't Look to the Kids for Validation

This is so important. If you look to the kids for your own sense of self-worth, there's a good chance you'll repeatedly find yourself in the pit of despair. They do not owe you anything. They do not owe you instant love, no matter how much you give them or do for them. They do not owe you loyalty or allegiance. And it is a mistake to expect instant love and acceptance the first month after you've married their father, no matter how long you've dated him before the wedding.

They do owe you respect as another human being on this planet. They do have to live by the boundaries of the household. But they do not have to like you. Instead, get your validation from your husband, your work, and your friends.

If the kids are showing resistance to getting close to you, back off. Relax. Let the relationship develop organically. Let it grow at its own pace. "I've seen the extremes a person will go to in order to get a kid to like them," says stepfamily counselor Bonnie Rudden of her years of helping new stepmoms. "They will overdo it, buying them things, doing things for the kids, and it usually ends up backfiring. Then the stepmom ends up saying, 'I've done all of this for you, and this is what you do to me?' But you've got to remember that kids are narcissistic and they'll take whatever you give them."

When you show a kid that you will bend over backward to get him to like you, you're giving him power over you and your marriage. Don't do that. Relationships are not made because you buy a kid something. They are made out of experiences and time spent together. If you let your insecurities about being liked rule you, your stepfamily development will suffer, not to mention your own sense of self-worth. If you value yourself, you don't need anyone else to tell you you're cool.

Sometimes stepmoms throw themselves into mothering their stepchildren because they've always wanted to be mothers, and if the kids don't respond well, it can be devastating. "If you've been waiting for marriage and kids your whole life, there's grief that your situation is not ideal. If you're not in touch with what's really going on with you, it's going to come out in ugly ways," says clinical social worker Patti Kelley Criswell. It's crucial to find out the motivations for your behavior.

Criswell acknowledges the strength it takes to be a stepmother who does not take things personally and does not look to her stepchildren for validation of her self-worth. "Stepmothers who do well are probably accomplished and very secure in who they are. To have unconditional positive regard for your stepchildren, it takes a damn secure woman to pull that off. She can say, 'I have the ability to meet my own emotional needs. It's not your job. I have my dog, my friends, my book club, my job.'"

If you do one small thing every day toward becoming a successful stepmother, wife, human being, you'll find that over time, you'll get to where you want to go even if it feels far away right now. Hang in there.

Brainstorming

If you're in the pit and don't see a way out of your current situation, find a group of people you can brainstorm with to find creative solutions. In my stepmom group, I left the first few meetings feeling depressed because everybody spent most of the time just venting anger and frustration. But once we all got the junk off our chests, we moved to the next phase, which was "Okay, so now that we've gotten that out, what do we do about it?"

Sally, who has four stepchildren between the ages of 7 and 16 living with her part-time in a two-bedroom apartment, said she didn't feel that she could come home from work and go into her room to read a book for a while to chill out without feeling bad.

Abe, her husband of two years, and his children would wonder what she was doing in there, so she would leave the door open. Without the door shut, however, she couldn't relax. But what if she negotiated? What if she told the kids and her husband she'd hang out with them after she spent half an hour letting go of her day behind her closed bedroom door? She tried it and it worked. Now they respect her need for some time and space, and when Sally comes out of her bedroom she is smiling instead of crabby.

Remember the Good

Take a moment and write a list of all the wonderful things you love about your stepkids. Funny things they've done or said. Touching moments. Write them down so you can remember them later when the going gets tough or they turn into teenagers.

Acceptance

Sometimes there is absolutely nothing you can do but ride it out. For instance, Stephanie moved in with an extremely troubled teenaged boy whose mother allowed him to stay out all night when he was 13 years old. After a brief stint of living with his mother, who didn't do much in the way of parenting, the boy chose to live with Dad and Stepmom, who demanded

he follow the rules of the house. But even though he de-
sired the boundaries his dad and stepmother set, he rebelled
against them by stealing things and drinking alcohol.

Stephanie maintained the rules of her house as best she
could. She even sacrificed her career as a college professor
by turning down an appointment at a new university—one
where she had long hoped to work—so her stepson could
finish high school. Eventually, Stephanie just had to accept
that this boy was deeply wounded long before he became her
stepson. That didn't mean Stephanie didn't do everything she
could to help; it just meant that she understood it was not
up to her what path this boy eventually chose to follow as he
entered adulthood.

I was one of those stepchildren who acted out. I have tattoos. I started smoking when I was 14 years old. I went out
with older boys. I was angry with everyone and didn't want
anyone telling me what to do, *especially* my stepparents. The
best thing all of my parents did for me (bio and step) was to
stay steady with the boundaries I couldn't cross and let me
find my way. Though my families both made a lot of mistakes
over the years, their steady show of support and their presence in my life eventually got through to me.

Now, most people I work with don't know I have tattoos or
that I used to smoke. They think I'm a happy, well adjusted,
successful woman with a fantastic home life—and they're
right. But it wasn't always that way.

When I think about the trials my own stepchildren will
have to go through, I know that some of it can be softened
by how their parents treat each other. I know I have a re-

sponsibility to be a healthy person who doesn't take out my insecurities on them. I know I can offer them support from my special role in their lives but that they aren't my kids, so there will always be a bit of a distance between us, even though I love them and want the best for them. I also know they are three individuals who will have to find their own way through life.

DISCUSSION TOPICS FOR TWO

1. How can we turn "It's not fair!" into "Let's work together"?
2. What can we do in our house to emphasize our family's strengths?
3. Whom can we go to for support? For comfort? For help?
4. What are ways we can rejuvenate ourselves? Our relationship? What things make us feel energized and hopeful? How can we plan our lives to include time apart and time together?
5. When we are unhappy with something going on in our stepfamily, how do we think our tension affects the children?

CHAPTER 10

All Work and No Play Makes Stepmom Wicked

The "I" Within "We"

CAREER GIRL'S PERSONAL ASSISTANT

1. Stay focused. What are the passions you want to maintain in your own life?
2. Make a commitment. How will you take care of yourself this week?
3. Schedule family time. When will you spend time with your family?
4. Keep connected. Have you communicated your needs to your spouse? Can you listen to his needs and work out a plan that also meets yours?

5. Maintain your energy. When you're feeling tired, it's often better to take a break than keep pushing yourself to perform. Can you be conscious of your energy levels and take breaks when you need to?

More women than ever before are educated, making greater amounts of money than their husbands and taking over what were traditionally male-dominated roles. That means it's even more important to find a balance between home and work life. Just because you're a new wife and step-mom doesn't mean you should neglect your career and passions while you're working to create a successful stepfamily.

When I married my husband, all of my hitched gal pals told me to expect the mysterious letdown that sets in after the drama of the big day—the postwedding blues that settle over the new bride and groom as they hash out who cleans the toilet and who pays the bills. But no one told me about the instant-family funk I'd be struck with after moving in with my husband and his three kids. There were so many things up in the air. My identity as a woman had changed; I was no longer single. And on top of everything, since I was successful in my work life, I thought I should know what to do at home. I should have been able to figure it all out quickly and efficiently. As it turns out, a business start-up is far easier than a stepfamily start-up.

"It helps if you let go of some of the perfection," says author Anne O'Connor. "A woman who is a professional in her job can say 'a, b, c, d' and it gets done, and she has a sense of accomplishment. She feels sharp and in control. She's talented and people respect her for those skills. And then she goes home, and she says '*a, b, c, d,*' and they go, 'No, we do *e, f, g, h* around here.' Suddenly everyone in her house has more say than she does."

There are some pretty common reactions to the fear caused by joining a stepfamily. Depending on your personality, you might throw yourself into life with the kids and give a great amount of your energy taking them to soccer practice and cooking dinner. You might try to love them and help them try to forget the pain of divorce. Or you might freak out and try to control what's happening to you by controlling all of these new people who are now in your space. You might try to enforce rules that you've lived by for years as you attempt to bend your new family to your will, but all in the spirit of helping them be better people, of course. You might try to be laid-back and a bit disengaged so you're not emotionally connecting with anyone in your new family.

However you jump into the chaos of early stepfamily life, if you are trying to help your stepchildren and your husband with nothing but the best intentions and you're met with rejection and rudeness, it hurts. It's a subtle reminder every time the kids don't look at you when they come into the room, or don't say hello to you, or direct questions at you only when they ask where Dad is. The daily onslaught of rejections can whittle away at even the most emotionally secure woman. Eventually, after working so hard, it feels as if you've got nothing left to give yourself.

Gretchen knows that feeling intimately. "What came first was the family structure. Second, my husband and I tried to focus on our relationship. Then my career, my work came in third for me or tied for second with my husband. And I came last. In the car driving to work was my own time, and work became my solitude because it was the only thing I had of my own. I went from one extreme to the other, from having everything my own to sharing everything."

Most stepfamily experts tell women who enter a stepfamily with no kids of their own to keep their own lives going in order to battle the instant-family funk. "It's a radical lifestyle change," says clinical social worker Patti Kelley Criswell. "If you look at someone who has a trauma that's outside their home, they want to stay home and nest. But in a stepfamily, the trauma is moving into a new home where everything is different. So a stepmother needs to do things that make her happy. This is a radical change, so if you really like your Monday night book group and Thursday night happy hour, then keep those things in place."

Lisa, a stepmom of two for the past twelve years, decided she would hit the books for her M.B.A. "I went back to school. I did that for myself, to have time for myself. Every night for two and a half years, I locked myself in my office to study for a couple of hours a day. I will still do that today, go to my little office and read, even though at eighteen and twenty the kids are older, they are moving on, doing their own thing. But I would take time for myself: I would work out, I would read, I would study, I would do that in my own space just to feel like I had some."

Even though two of Georgianne's stepkids don't live with her full-time anymore, all four children regularly visit. Georgianne makes sure she gets together with her girlfriends and spends time on her own. "I have a good solid group of girl-friends and we all went through transitions at the same time, but we still make an effort to get together for girls' night every few months. On Saturday mornings I go off for the day. I go to the movies and take myself out for lunch, and that helps me feel renewed and ready for anything."

Anne O'Connor agrees that women need to have their own lives to stay sane and feel confident in a situation that can easily make you feel less-than. "Women in this situation who don't have children of their own, put their whole selves into trying to make this work. Then they get resentful when it doesn't happen. It's going to take work over the long haul. Get something you do for yourself all the time—a class, a walk, yoga, aerobics. Go do something that is yours, that is your own life, even if only for an hour a day, so you don't forget who you are."

In our household, when we were first learning how to live and be together, I clung to my hobbies and passions so I would feel that I was still me in the middle of so much change. I rewarded myself with massages, exercise, and lunches with my pals. My old routines and habits became life preservers, helping me remember that though my surroundings had changed, I was still me.

Work It Out

Your work life can help keep your confidence up since you're doing something you know you're good at. "Work is an important part of me. It's a part of my identity and makes me a more fulfilled person," says Marie, who decided to continue climbing the corporate ladder. At 35, she's an account manager and media relations director at an advertising agency. She has a 21-year-old stepson she met when he was 9, and two children under age 5 with her husband, Grant.

Lauren is a doctor who married Tom when she was 24 years old, and twenty-five years later, they are still married. Tom was the junior vice president of a bank and had full custody of three boys. Then the couple had three more boys together. Yet even with so much going on at home, Lauren's career was important to her. "I stayed very career-focused, and because I spent more than a hundred hours a week at the hospital, that was really my life. My family life would weave in and out of my work. My husband worked full-time, but he had most of the job of picking up his kids."

The family was fortunate enough to have a housekeeper, so when Lauren did get home, she could spend quality time with her family instead of having to pitch in on household chores. Now she no longer works, but she's glad she had her career: "I needed it for my own ego and identity and self-worth."

My career has evolved from writing stories on yellow legal pads when I was a kid to writing for a living. My professional life has as much impact on my well-being as my home life does. If I never picked up a pen again, it would be bad for me and for my family; it's much better for all of us that I'm doing something I love. I am more able to be present and involved at home and not let the little things bother me because my work sustains me.

Me, Me, Me-Time

Just like chocolate and red wine, too much of a good thing is not always good for you. You must find the balance between getting time for yourself doing things you love and creating a marriage and stepfamily that works for all of you. All along I have stressed the importance of your relationship with your husband. Healthy me-time can become unhealthy if it replaces the time you spend with your spouse when the stepfamily terrain becomes more challenging.

"All of a sudden the Prince Charming falls off his horse and turns into the pal, the defender, the white knight of the little beasts that are jumping up and down on the stepmother's white couch," says Jeannette Lofas, founder of Stepfamily Foundation, Inc., headquartered in New York City. "She says, 'That's my white couch,' and he says, 'He's just expressing himself. Why are you being so excessive?' Then this woman goes to the office for long hours and on weekends. She may give up and withdraw and go get her nails done or see her girlfriends rather than being present for the children's visits. A common misconception of successful women is, 'If I try harder, I'll succeed.' But that can lead to depression. Instead, she has to work smarter."

Find ways to manage the daily stressors by exploring healthy channels for your anger. If things are not working as well as you hoped with your stepkids, you're going to need other things to focus on. This is true of any parent, not just stepparents. You've got to have your own life and maintain your ties to your home at the same time.

My husband, Arne, had this insight about women who marry men with children: "It's a completely different way of life. You don't have the freedom to go out and have a cup of coffee or run out and see a movie or do things you've normally done. One instinct may be to go out and do things by yourself, but that can send a message that you're uninterested or don't want to participate. Besides hurting your spouse's feelings by making him feel as if you don't want to be involved, that message can be conveyed to the kids and they pick up on that, too."

So what is your happy medium? How can you make sure to do things for yourself, still give time and energy to your marriage, and spend one-on-one time with your stepkids, all while juggling your career?

In our house, we have the kids 50 percent of the time. On the days we don't have the kids, my husband and I plan our date nights or trips so we can spend time together doing activities we both enjoy. When we do have the kids, we spend time doing things as a family, such as a trip to the park or swimming at the health club, and then we split off so we can each spend alone time with the kids. I might take one grocery shopping with me while my husband takes two to the park. Or he will take one to breakfast and I'll take two on a walk with the dog to pick up muffins and juice.

I rotate my alone time and evenings out with friends so they sometimes occur when we have the kids and sometimes don't. Then no one feels left out, and I still get to have those nights that energize me. I also have a ton of afternoon coffee dates and lunches with friends because that way I don't miss out on evening time with my family.

Go Lightly

Sometimes I mess it all up. Sometimes I'm gone too much and the kids start asking about why I'm never there, or I stay home too much and we all get cranky. Sometimes I try to fix things and can't. Occasionally I get involved where I shouldn't. Other times I let things go and figure they'll just have to work themselves out. Most of the time I genuinely do the best I can, but sometimes that means staying in bed with the door closed listening to music so I don't hear anything but what I want to hear. And that's okay, too. Then I can get up in the morning and start fresh.

Get to Know You

There's nothing like conflict to help you delve into the depths of yourself to find out why you do and feel things. There are many opportunities for growth and grace in a stepfamily, and sometimes the inner work you have to do is absolutely no fun. But it's worth it. With books such as *The Purpose-Driven Life: What on Earth Am I Here For?* by Rick Warren topping the bestseller charts, it's clear that people do want to feel as if they are here on this planet for a reason. As a stepmother, you're going to affect those children's lives. Someday they will do things that you didn't even realize you taught them. They'll say things the way you say them. They'll decide to go to a particular college because you told them you thought it was a good idea. You're going to have an impact on those children. What do you want it to be?

Your Own Path

When I was a kid, it was a war zone in both of my houses, not only before and during my parents' divorce but for years afterward. Back then, my friends would ask me if I imagined getting married and moving in with a handsome man. I would answer, sure I want to get married, but I have to live next door to my spouse. I want a beautiful glass tunnel to connect our houses, but I want my own house.

Arne wasn't into that idea when we got married, but he very much appreciates the fact that we both have our individual lives to lead. We have a huge influence on each other, there's no doubt, but at the end of the day, I die alone. I am the one who must justify my actions. I need to feel that my life is important and that I have a purpose here. I know my purpose includes my marriage and helping guide my stepchildren into adulthood. I also need to fulfill those things I think I myself was put here to do.

I walk the line between being completely and fully committed to my marriage and being able to do the things I feel called to do on my own. I want both the "I" and the "we." What about you?

DISCUSSION TOPICS FOR TWO

1. Do we both feel like Stepmom is around often enough and participating in our stepfamily life?
2. What about Dad? When does he get a break?
3. How much time away from the family is too much?
4. What are our top five values in life? Passions? What do we think is most important?
5. Make a list of the hundred things you want to do before you die. Then share the lists with each other to see what things you have in common and what things you must do alone.
6. Is it okay for us to be "I" and how does that fit into "we"?

CHAPTER 11

• •

Community Relations

Stepmotherhood Changes Your Relationships

CAREER GIRL'S PERSONAL ASSISTANT

1. Set career goals. Identify what you want out of your career in the short run and for the long term.
2. Brainstorm creative solutions. If you and your partner have his kids full-time, can you afford a nanny? Is there a family friend who can come over and help you clean the house? How can you and your spouse find creative solutions to running the house so your career doesn't suffer?
3. Define your objectives. If you keep your family informed about what's happening with your career, they

can become your cheering section. Do your spouse and stepkids know why your career is important to you?

4. **Be aware of office politics.** Stepmoms don't get maternity leave when they marry a man with kids, but the emotional upheaval can be just as challenging to deal with as having a new baby. Confidence goes a long way to help you maintain your relationships with your colleagues. Can you be upfront about your new responsibilities without sacrificing what you've worked so hard to build?

5. **Watch for burnout.** Magazines are filled with tips to help women juggle work and home life because it's a chronic problem. How will you avoid burning out from trying to perform well at work and within your family unit?

Most of us care what other people think about us at least to some degree, and the fact that the myth of the wicked stepmother still informs most people's views of stepmotherhood is pretty distressing—especially considering there are more than 15 million of us in the United States. That's a lot of women who are rowing upstream to overcome a negative stereotype perpetuated by stories of horrible stepmothers who torture their stepchildren.

It's not only fairy tales that perpetuate the image of the wicked stepmother. Kim Leon and Erin Angst published "Portrayals of Stepfamilies in Film: Using Media Images in Remarriage Education" in the January 2005 issue of *Family Relations*. The authors sifted through thousands of movies and found that in films portraying stepfamilies, 73 percent were judged to have a negative tone.

It seems ridiculous to have to worry that you might belong to a group of women considered "evil" or "wicked" merely because you married that man. And yet when I watched *Ever After: A Cinderella Story* with my stepchildren, after a scene showcasing the stepmother's wickedness, my stepson said, "Thank goodness you're not like that." Am I truly a good stepmom—or is that only by comparison to Cinderella's? What does this negative perception do to our ability to succeed as stepmothers? How does it impact other people's perceptions of us?

Colleagues

Here are some responses from colleagues that a new stepmother might get when she says "I'm a stepmother" or "I have X many stepkids."

- They blow it off with an "Oh, that's nice," and then never ask you about your family again because it makes them uncomfortable.
- They begin asking you highly inappropriate and intimate questions about how your husband ended his last marriage and whether or not you were involved in the breakup.
- They assume you are just like a mother, and therefore will ask you all sorts of questions about your stepkids

that you may or may not know the answer to because, after all, you're not their mother.

- They don't understand how you, a formerly single pal who constantly worked late hours, suddenly can't because you have to go home to participate in the ritual-building stepfamily dinner. They aren't even your kids, so why do you have to leave?

Stepmotherhood could have a negative impact on your career. One stepmother recalls a conversation with a boss who told her he hated hiring women of a certain age because when they got married and had children, they inevitably either quit or asked to work fewer hours. When he found out she was becoming a stepmother, he made a joke about how the quality and quantity of her work would decline. Not funny.

Because there are no hard-and-fast rules about stepmotherhood, everyone in a new stepmom's community of co-workers will have a different opinion about what it means. Just as you must at home, you have to decide what your boundaries will be at work. When my colleagues who are mothers of young children ask me questions they feel every mother must know about their children, I say, "I'm not their mother. I'm their stepmother. It's different."

Gretchen remembers being highly offended at her colleagues' assumptions that she wasn't as committed to her family as she would be if her stepchildren were her biological children. "The attitudes of people have always surprised me. Most people outside the family unit have a hard time thinking you're a family unit. They say things like 'The kids are only with you half of the time. That must be nice. But they're not your kids—why do you miss them so much?'"

Gretchen also struggled with meeting the requirements of her high-profile job at the same time that she was an active parenting figure to her two stepchildren. "I don't know that executive women get the support they need. People still frown when you're leaving early for a kid's thing, whether they're your kids or your stepkids. And so you feel like you always have to choose."

Joining a new stepfamily is a crucial time for you to assess what your career goals are for the next five, ten, and fifteen years. You must look honestly at how this dynamic will change your working habits. When I became a stepmother, my work life changed instantly. I could no longer work until midnight. Instead, I had a family demanding my attention as soon as they walked in the door at 5:30 P.M. For a while I went along with it, until I realized I was becoming more resentful every time my work was interrupted. I had to consciously decide what my hours would be and adjust my work habits to complement my new lifestyle.

So how can a stepmom who is involved in building a new stepfamily maintain the respect and relationships she's developed in her career? "To me, it all comes down to confidence," says Darcy, stepmom of two and a human resources manager. "The one thing you can do to ensure failure is to show your indecision or weakness. You have to have confidence if you're going to have people trust you and follow your lead."

All in the Family

A woman may also find that her family isn't supportive of her new marriage because no parent ever dreams that a daughter will grow up to join a stepfamily. "I was young and naïve and it was a time in my life where I didn't really know anything but success, so I kind of assumed everything would work out," recalls Lauren, the doctor who met her husband and his three sons when she was 21. "I got an awful lot of concern and advice from my mother and my family that this was going to be difficult. There was a long time where my mother tried to get me to discontinue the relationship. Like most young people, I didn't listen to her warnings." Even though it may have hurt Lauren's feelings when her mother didn't support her new relationship, it's also easy to see why her mother would have tried to protect her from entering into a relationship that would have more difficulties than if she'd dated a man without children. Lauren would have an instant family since her husband-to-be had full custody of his three boys. Their mother lived out of state and had inconsistent contact with the children.

Debra was terrified to tell her family about the man she'd met and started dating at work. Jake was divorced and had two young girls. "We waited a while before I told anyone we were dating, which is rare for me, because my family, we're always together. My family always knows everything I'm doing, and it was a few months before they even knew it. I told them on Thanksgiving Day with a glass of red wine in one hand and a cup of coffee in the other. My dad is my role model, and he flipped out like my worst nightmare. He teared up and walked out of the room.

"I thought it was because Jake was divorced and had kids, but it was because I worked with him. Two hours later my dad came back and said, 'I can tell you're really happy, and I'm happy for you; I just want to make sure you've thought about your career.' That was his main concern. I'm sure he had concerns about the stepkids, but that's my father. I was this career person. Right out of my M.B.A. program, I worked. I traveled the world. Everything I did was my job."

When you walk down the aisle with your husband, not only do you enter into a family with children, you also get in-laws. It could be that a stepmom's new in-laws won't know how to act around her, especially if no one in their family has ever been divorced. They may treat her as they treated their son's first wife. They may be resentful. They might decide they want to stay in contact with their son's ex. Or your husband's ex might still be in contact with some of his family members, which can create divisions of loyalty among your husband's family. If your husband's family is having difficulty knowing how to act, encourage your husband to talk to them privately and to express his needs.

It's important for a new stepmom and her spouse to outline the ways they will deal with extended family members together. Just as you and your husband must hash out how you will approach the children and living together, you must also figure out how you will handle your parents in a way that makes you both feel supported and understood.

Sandy was close with her in-laws during her first marriage but decided that she was not willing to extend herself like that the second time around. "In your first marriage, you send all the birthday cards and Christmas cards to his family and you try very hard to be a good daughter-in-law," she says. "In my second marriage, he sends his own cards. My relationship is with him, not them. None of his family live here. We're friendly, but it's not close."

Stacy recalls how her new in-laws welcomed her with open arms. But at the same time, they constantly told her stories of her spouse's days with his ex-wife. Ouch. As a stepmother, you might have moments with your new extended family that make you feel incredibly uncomfortable. Presumably they want the best for their son, and if he's smiling, they're happy.

Best Friends Forever

When Eleanor left her life as a chef in New York City to move to the Midwest, where she married her husband and gained two young stepsons, her friends could not understand her decision. "I got such negative flak from people. They all asked me, 'Why are you doing that?'" Eleanor recalls. She'd been living the high life in the Big Apple, and children weren't a part of her paradigm.

Losing her single friends was the biggest blow to Marie when she got serious with a man thirteen years her senior with a son from a previous marriage. She was 23 when they met and 27 when they married. "It was really difficult for me when my gang of friends stopped calling. When all of your single friends call you up and say, 'Yeah, we're going to a movie tonight,' and you say you have to be home early to spend time with your boyfriend and his kid because that's where you *want* to spend your time, they stop calling. I lost my identity as a single friend with all of my girlfriends. That caused me some really sad moments."

Laura, a corporate attorney, remembers how her single pals didn't call her anymore when she married, gained a young stepdaughter, and moved to the suburbs. "It's a huge transition," she says. "When your friends are all single women and you go and get married, you lose touch with them. I was friends with a group of really bitter single women, and once I wasn't one of them anymore, I was cast out of the circle. I had moved to the suburbs, where, essentially, I knew no one. I spent the first three months we lived there being miserable."

Mary, on the other hand, found an entire community of people she would never have connected with if it weren't for her five stepchildren. "I'm pretty extroverted, so I like being with people. And it's fun being part of the community like you're a parent. I meet so many people at school events and church whom I wouldn't have met otherwise. Your circle grows immensely when there are kids."

Place of Worship

For many Americans, their place of worship is where they find refuge. To feel silenced in the one place they come looking for solace leads stepfamilies deeper underground. A common story told by members of the clergy—and therapists, too, by the way—is that a couple will come seeking help but not state they're in a stepfamily until after several meetings. How can a professional give help to stepfamilies when we won't even admit we're in them?

Mary has five stepchildren, but she doesn't consider herself their parent. Though she started dating their father, Pat, when the kids were all young, she didn't marry him until most of them were out of the house. Still, she struggles with what to do when she goes to church on Mother's Day. "I hate Mother's Day. We should have Stepmom's Day. In church on Mother's Day they all stand up, and I just can't get up. And people will say, 'But you're just like their mother—you've done so much for them,' but no, I am not."

Judy is devout and is honored she's played a role in guiding her stepchildren to being more spiritual people. And though she is actively involved at her church helping other couples, she says it's sometimes hard to feel at home at a church because stepfamilies are left out. "It's a subtle thing and I don't think people in churches intentionally reject stepfamilies, stepchildren, stepmoms, or stepdads. I do think they're neglectful and forgetful of the uniqueness of the challenges that people have in those situations."

As the marriage education movement grows across the country, more religious groups are offering stepfamily education classes than ever before. Divorce is no longer considered the stigma it once was, and so there are more resources for remarried couples. If you feel left out at your place of worship, say something to the leaders about what you'd like to hear. What if the pastor on Mother's Day asked all the moms, stepmoms, grandmas, adoptive moms, and women who care for children to stand up? And how about the same message of acceptance for all the different kinds of dads on Father's Day?

School

Teachers and school officials are getting smarter about how to handle stepfamilies, but there is still much education to be done so stepfamilies are given positive support. In many schools, contact sheets still only have room for Mom and Dad's contact information with no room for Stepmom or Stepdad. Neglect could come in the form of a teacher who assumes every child needs only one conference at which both parents will show up. It could be that a child is given only two tickets to graduation.

Since grade-school kids don't like to be labeled as different, teachers who are inclusive of stepfamilies can help a child's sense of self-confidence. For instance, Stacy, a CEO of a publicity agency, reports that her youngest stepdaughter brought her a homemade Mother's Day gift from school that had "Mommy" written on it. The little girl's mother also got one. The teacher had told the children to make gifts for their mothers, and since this little girl wanted to give her stepmother a gift but didn't want to stand out by asking the teacher if that was okay, she didn't admit she had a stepmother. Instead, she said she'd messed up the first present so she could make another.

It can be awkward for stepmoms to show up at school functions, whether Mom is there or not. It's not only uncomfortable for you and your husband and his ex and her new husband, but for other parents, too. My stepmother was not involved in my school life because she figured that was my mother's place. And now that my stepmom has her own daughter in school, she can appreciate both sides. "When you're married and have a child, most of your couple friendships come from work, your child's school, your church, or your neighborhood. More than half of our couple friends and my girlfriends are parents of my daughter's friends," says Nancy. "If you're a stepmom, it's hard to fit in with that. It makes people nervous when there are two different couples with the same child."

There are, of course, exceptions to this common experience. Some stepmothers become the primary caregivers of their stepchildren and participate in all of the school activities. It depends on all the variables you've got going in your family dynamic. Is Mom around? Is she active at their school? Are you and she on good terms?

I'd be willing to bet that if you don't feel uncomfortable and self-conscious about your status as a stepmother, then other people won't feel awkward about it either.

It could take a while for you to figure out what your level of involvement is going to be with the kids' school. You've got to learn what your stepchildren, husband, and the other household all feel comfortable with, too. If Mom has left the kids and moved to another state, then you may be asked to go to conferences and help out in homeroom. If Mom has always been a big part of her children's school lives, it might be best if you show up only at the concerts and games.

At school, at family gatherings, at your place of worship, and at work, the way you face the world as a stepmother can help put the fairy tales and wicked stereotypes to rest once and for all.

DISCUSSION TOPICS FOR TWO

1. What do we think of when we hear the term "stepmother"? What images come to mind? What qualities? Can you be subversive and create a fairy tale with a good stepmother?
2. How can we develop a system of social support that gives us positive messages instead of negative ones about stepparenting and stepfamilies?
3. What do you need to communicate to your colleagues or boss? How will you manage your career now that you have stepchildren?
4. Are there people who make us feel self-conscious about being a stepfamily?
5. What do we need from our jobs, place of worship, or children's school to help us feel accepted?

CHAPTER 12

The Other Woman

Coming to Terms with the Ex

CAREER GIRL'S PERSONAL ASSISTANT

1. **Set a meeting.** When's the best time to meet the biological mother of your stepchildren? That depends. If you've been in your stepchildren's lives and they talk about you all the time, Mom may request a meeting. Some women meet for the first time at school functions. Others don't meet until after an engagement or wedding. Monica is a financial planner who didn't meet her stepdaughter's mom until her stepdaughter married, even though she'd been her stepmother for more than a decade. What feels like the best time to meet her to you?

2. **Decide on your approach.** What do you hope for your relationship with your stepkids' bio mom? What do you think is appropriate? Will you be okay if she rejects any advances you make?

3. **Focus on the kids.** Make the children the focus of your conversations. Unless you become friends, can you keep discussions on topics related to the children?

4. **Be respectful.** This relationship can be incredibly awkward. What will you do to make it easier for everyone involved? Sometimes that means staying out of the middle of things. Sometimes that could mean becoming an active parenting partner with her. Can you understand how she might be feeling?

5. **Exit strategy.** If you and she can't get along, it's best to minimize the tension any way you can for the sake of the kids. How will you gracefully decline from participating in any drama?

You've probably dated and dumped or been dumped by other partners during the course of your life. You may even have married before but chose to end it before kids came along. And though occasionally an old boyfriend might turn up to see what you're up to, it's sporadic. Those former flames usually don't come back to your life to haunt you. Not so for your husband and his ex. As parents, they are joined together for the rest of their lives. That means as the new wife, you also have to learn to deal with this other woman.

The first time I met my husband's ex he was still living in the house they once shared. Though she didn't live there anymore, she still knew the code to the garage door. Arne and I were making out when we heard the sound of the garage door going up.

"What is that?" I asked, scrambling to put myself back together.

Arne swore, jumped up and ran to intercept his ex. When I went downstairs, hair disheveled and cheeks flushed, she was standing there in the kitchen gathering up things the kids had forgotten to take with them to her apartment and asking Arne if there were any stamps left. Instantly, I felt as if I was 16 years old and had just been busted by my parents. I felt as if I had done something wrong.

The second time we met, even though I was prepared, I still felt awkward and self-conscious. And now that we've spent time together on a soccer field and exchanged pleasantries in passing, we're polite but don't really know each other.

There are many ways to handle the relationship you'll have with your husband's ex-wife. Some stepmoms and bio moms have become best friends. Some handle each other socially as though they were polite acquaintances, and others have incredible confrontational moments. Whatever type of relationship a stepmother ends up in with a bio mom, it's rarely easy, no matter how good it looks on the surface.

"I would try to sympathize and see her side of things," reports Catherine, an actress, whose husband, James, has a 14-year-old son and an ex-wife who lives a block away. "I have really tried in my personal dealings with her to be civil. It takes its toll because it's not what I really feel. Inside, I am thinking, 'I don't trust you at all.' I find her an incredibly manipulative person and I get really upset when I see her manipulating a situation. Then I get defensive of my husband, and then I get frustrated with him for letting her call all the shots."

For stepmothers across the country, dealing with the ex-wife is one of the most challenging aspects of the new marriage. Often there is immediate antagonism, even if the two have never met and the first marriage has been over for a long time. Especially if an affair between you and your new mate led to the breakup of the first marriage, you could be in for a war with the ex that could play out for decades, often at the expense of the children.

On the flip side, some biological moms and stepmoms get along famously. Darcy married Jud in 1999. At the time he had two children, ages 7 and 11, from his previous marriage. Darcy hit it off so well with her husband's ex that she asked her stepchildren's mother to be the godmother of the first child she had with her husband.

All of the latest research about children of divorce indicates that when a child gets into a stepfamily, whether a remarriage has taken place or a parent is living with another adult, children exhibit far fewer risky behaviors if the conflict between former spouses and between households is minimal. So whether you're buddies with your husband's ex or not, as a new stepmother in this complex family system, you've got to take responsibility for making things run smoothly. Strive for a relationship with your stepchildren's mother that is calm and respectful, and keep the best interests of the children center stage.

Jealousy

When I first started dating Arne, a friend of mine took me aside about a month into my new relationship and gave me what I thought at the time was strange advice.

"Don't freak out when he calls you his ex-wife's name," she said.

"Yeah, right," I scoffed. I couldn't begin to imagine it. No man had ever called me anything but my own name. My ego reeled at the thought. My friend had been married for ten years to a man who had previously been married for twenty-five years to another woman, and was speaking from experience. "It's nothing personal," my friend continued. "And he'll feel really bad about it."

Her words haunted me for weeks. After all, the man of my dreams was divorced after a ten-year marriage that lasted most of his twenties and into his early thirties and included three children. He'd spent more than a decade saying *her* name. I had attended a women's college and was trained to support and love my female sisters, but I found that the mere fact of her existence filled me with hostility. My feelings had nothing to do with her personality or any of our interactions. I was simply upset because she was wife number one, and if Arne and I decided to get married, I would be wife number two.

Here's the ugly truth: I was jealous. Even though I was the owner of my own business, a world traveler, a chic, sophisticated woman of the world, I felt like a spoiled little girl who found out her sister has already played with her new toy. "But that's mine!"

After my friend's warning, I half expected to hear the ex's name at some point and was almost listening for it.

Then it happened. We were talking one evening a few months after we met when I heard the name that wasn't my own. My chest hurt. I didn't move. Couldn't move. Couldn't breathe.

Rationally, I could work it out. He was with this other woman for more than ten years. Lived with her every single day. Had kids with her. Paid bills with her. He was used to saying her name. He still coparented with her. I knew I couldn't punish him for this, even though a part of me wanted to see him suffer. For a moment I imagined how good it would feel to make him listen to explicit stories about every man I'd ever dated. But when he turned to me with tears on his face, I knew there was nothing I could do to make him feel worse than he already felt.

We cried in each other's arms and wondered if things could ever be the same between us. I didn't know if I could feel safe again. I started to tense up every time he said my name, waiting for the hurt. Expecting it. Guarding against it.

The next time I saw him he said, "I love you, Jacque."

"That's right, say my name, bitch!" I yelled, calling out the line from the movie *American Pie,* in which the lead character, a high school senior, is dating a girl who is a bit aggressive when he loses his virginity to her on prom night. In the funny scene, she demands he say her name.

Arne looked at me a bit shocked, and then we both howled with laughter. I won't lie: It still makes my skin crawl to think about that moment. For a while, we even made a pact that we were only allowed to use pet names for each other to ensure we both felt completely safe. And the hilarious names we came up with kept us light-hearted and ever more confident in our love.

Now when I feel envious or jealous, I send thoughts of gratitude to the ex for teaching him to put the toilet seat down—and for letting him go. I know that Arne loves Jacque. That he knows how to spell it correctly. That he knows my middle name and how much I weigh.

The moral of the story? Let go of the jealousy any way you can. It's corrosive to your insides and your marriage. Find a way to laugh, to change the downward spiral of your thoughts midstream. Here's a completely ludicrous exercise to try. I've done it and it's so stupid, it actually works. It was beginning to feel as if there was a track in my brain that the ugly, jealous thoughts, once started, would just run along, as though they were recordings. I wondered what would happen if I disrupted the flow of negative thoughts with a nonsensical word that would jar me out of the cycle. My youngest stepdaughter was wearing a shirt with a pineapple on it that day. So I started saying "pineapple" to myself every time I started feeling jealous, and it was so ridiculous I ended up laughing every time. The good news is that it worked.

Finding Your Place

Figuring out your relationship with the ex will happen over time. But my advice is don't push it. No matter how wonderful or kind or manipulative or horrible you think she is, you've got to respect her position as mother to your stepchildren. Remember this: Those lovely attributes your stepchildren exhibit don't *all* come from your husband's influence.

My own stepmother, Nancy, put this concept very eloquently. "I had a great appreciation early on for the decency, warmth, and sense of humor that you and your brothers had and I always knew a huge part of that was your mom. I could see a lot of good things in all three of you that were less likely from your dad because he was gone so much."

It can be hard for new stepmothers to respect mom's place in her children's lives. In fact, according to a study called "Contesting the Myth of the 'Wicked Stepmother,'" published in the *Western Journal of Communication* by Allison Christian, a professor at the University of Denver, stepmothers sometimes combat the myth of the wicked stepmother by slamming the biological mother to make themselves feel better. But I contend that if you harbor anger at your stepchildren's mother, it's only going to hurt you, your husband, and your stepchildren. Mom is a part of the picture whether you like it or not, so do everything you can to make peace with that concept.

Among stepmothers, the topic of attending school conferences is hotly contested. The women who spend hours studying with the children at the kitchen table insist they have a right to be at the school conferences, regardless of whether or not the biological moms feel comfortable having them there. In a few cases, women I interviewed mentioned that the bio mom had requested they not be at the conference, but they went anyway.

If you're involved in a high-conflict stepfamily where the two households don't negotiate well and Mom is uncomfortable with your presence at the school conference, then schedule another one with the teacher. What's the big deal? Teachers, just like clergy and therapists, are seeing more stepfamilies every day, and they should already know that some families need two meetings per kid.

But if you demand to be highly involved in your stepchildren's lives, consider whom you are hurting when you show up at the conference or the graduation or the wedding with no regard for Mom's wishes: the kids. The kids get the brunt of your actions every single time in one way or another. Perhaps Mom then calls Dad and freaks out at him, and then Dad is in a pissy mood and takes it out on the kids. At the very least, the kids will certainly pick up on the tension between you and Mom in the tone of your voice or even your body language when you talk about their mother. When you do something in a stepfamily to rock the boat, the effects are felt across the entire family system—for a long time.

I'm not saying you shouldn't go to your stepchild's wedding, because you belong there if your stepchild wants you there. But please think strategically about your involvement in your stepchild's life, especially when Mom's behavior isn't exemplary. Consider all the angles. Be as flexible as possible if you need to rearrange schedules, and try to take the burden off the kids if you can.

Weddings are notorious for the emotions they bring up. Monica, the financial planner, has been married to Ben, the father of a grown daughter, for eleven years. She dated him for four years before they got married. Her husband had been married for twenty-five years and was in the middle of his divorce when they met. Monica had never met his ex until her stepdaughter married. Before the wedding, Monica's mother gave her this advice: "You're the stepmother. Your job is to wear beige and smile." Harsh! But the sentiments are right on. A stepmother's place at a wedding is to ask her stepchildren what they want her to do and to take a back seat to Mom.

In the weeks before the wedding, Monica's stepdaughter did everything she could think of to make sure her mother was taken care of, because her mother was notorious for throwing tantrums. She expected her to flip out on the big day and even asked her dad not to stand in the receiving line to make Mom happy. When Monica did finally meet the ex, the woman was rude. Monica worked hard to be gracious and supportive of her stepdaughter, even though the woman's behavior hurt her and her husband. Monica knew if she made a scene, her step-daughter would be the one to shoulder the burden.

Mum's the Word

I've said this before, but it bears repeating: Do not bad-mouth the ex to the children. As tempted as you may be sometimes, it's a definite no-no. No matter what the age of the child or his relationship to his mother, whether she's remarried, deceased, or has abandoned him, you must not bad-mouth his mother.

Here's what typically happens when stepmoms don't follow this rule. A kid might feel protective of and loyal toward his mother and will hate you because she's his mother. Or, your stepdaughter might feel that your judgment of her mother is a slam about her. Since the child is an extension of her mother, you must hate *her*, too.

If Mom is still around and involved in your stepchildren's lives, it's not your place to get in the middle, no matter how rocky their relationship. Don't trash-talk her in front of the kids, even if you disapprove of her new husband or the lifestyle she chooses at her house. Just don't do it. It will blow up in your face.

Fifteen-year-old Nicole and her stepmother, Kathleen, said they actually do talk honestly about the bio mom's shortcomings because they are such good friends. Still, with such a strong relationship, they can talk about Mom only to a point. If this stepdaughter feels that her stepmother is attacking her mother instead of just offering neutral advice, she will come to her mother's defense every time. Well, wouldn't you?

The Smart Steps class for stepfamilies by Francesca Adler-Baeder, distributed by the National Stepfamily Resource Center, lays down only a few absolute don'ts, but this is on the list, ladies: *Don't bad-mouth the ex*.

That goes even if she does something that Judy's husband's ex did. "The first thing my stepchildren's bio mom did after my husband and I were married was to take them to see *Cinderella*. I decided to graciously assume that was an unconscious intention, but it was inappropriate."

Instead, blow off steam about the ex to your pals or

your stepmom support group. Ask for help brainstorming strategies to deal with her—but keep your frustrations from the kids. By the way, bad-mouthing Mom to your husband can also backfire. If your husband thinks you're judging him for marrying her in the first place, he might defend his ex to you, and that can put a gap between you and him. Do talk to your husband about your feelings, but tread carefully. Some things are better left unsaid.

In the Spotlight

As much as possible, stay out of the middle of your husband's relationship with the ex. He should be the one communicating with her. Why take on a burden that isn't yours? I know you want to help, but overall, it's better if you stay out of their relationship. Talk to your husband and work through decisions together behind the scenes so you feel comfortable, but let him be the one onstage.

Beth learned that the hard way. Her husband was divorced for ten years when they married. He had one child from his previous marriage, and Beth knew going in that this was a high-conflict situation. "When I first met him, he told me all about his ex and how he couldn't have girlfriends because she always chased them away. The first time I met his ex-wife, she was screaming and yelling at him. Then she screamed in my face. After we got married, my husband and his ex-wife would fight so badly that it was miserable for everybody, so I would try to do the mediating. That didn't work."

For a while, Beth and her stepdaughter's stepfather did the communicating between households, but that ended up not working either. The whole group ended up back in court-ordered mediation. Eventually Beth's stepdaughter was old enough to tell her parents what she was and was not willing to do, but the child is the one who suffered.

Gretchen helped her family by stepping into the role of communicator with the other household. But because the ex was verbally abusive to her, Gretchen insisted that all communications were to be either faxed or e-mailed. No phone calls happened between any of the adults in this stepfamily unit.

The Bad Guy

In her book *Becoming a Stepfamily: Patterns of Development in Remarried Families*, Patricia Papernow advises therapists working with stepfamilies to make sure they do not side with one member in a stepfamily and make the other side the "bad guy" because everyone has a compelling story to tell. For stepmoms involved in nasty relations with the former wife, it can be easy to turn Mom into the villain. In fact, except for a very few, all of the stepmothers I interviewed had something bad to say about the ex. But people just aren't that black and white. Moms are people, too.

Remember when you were a kid and you were always told to try to see things from another person's point of view? You might have heard things such as "When you said that to your friend, how do you think that made her feel?" We're still on the playground when it comes to learning about stepfamily dynamics. If there is a disruption at the other house, always consider what it must be like for Mom to send her children off to (in most cases) a virtual stranger, leaving her with absolutely no control and no say about what is happening to her children. I doubt I could be as gracious as my husband's ex if I were in her shoes.

If you helped bust up your husband's marriage to his ex, are you surprised she's not taking kindly to your advances? You may feel guilty for the rest of your life, but that's your cross to bear. Stay away from Mom, smile and nod and don't expect to ever get any nods back from her. Be sensitive when you attend events, and stay home if it's too tense. With time, the tension may fade and you can all be in the same room together. If you can't be in the same room without a scene, again consider what that is doing to the kids. Your relationship with them will suffer every time your mere presence makes Mom cry. Be gracious. Go get your nails done or hang with your inner posse so you can feel supported and loved in the middle of a tough situation.

If you've had a good relationship with your husband's ex up until the engagement was announced or the wedding day approached or a new baby arrived, don't be surprised if your relations take a nosedive for a while, and maybe permanently. One stepmother reported that her working relationship with her husband's ex exploded in her face when her husband announced they were getting married. The ex freaked out again the week of their wedding; this time she yelled at her former husband about a series of unrelated issues. If your husband's ex is not remarried, expect the responses to the big pivotal events in your life to be even more dramatic. Put yourself in her shoes and you might be able to empathize with her. Even though 85 percent of divorces are sought by women, it doesn't mean the ex won't have feelings about her former husband marrying another woman. It's the big finale, the end of the dream, for real.

Boundaries

I know I sound pretty tough on stepmoms in this chapter, and I mean to be. It takes a lot of maturity to be a successful stepmom. But you can do it. Setting up your boundaries with the ex can help you feel strong in a situation that is loaded with the potential to make you feel stripped of power.

Sandy had to set a boundary with her husband around phone calls. One night after she and her husband, Tim, were intimate and still in bed together, the phone rang, and her husband answered. It was his ex. And instead of telling her he'd call her back later, he proceeded to have a twenty-minute conversation with her. Sandy was enraged that he would let the ex interrupt their special time together without a thought about her feelings. That moment was this couple's impetus to begin setting boundaries.

Another lament I hear a lot from stepmoms who don't have sturdy boundaries with the ex is, "There's another woman in my marriage!" But the fact is, she's not in your marriage. The only people in your marriage are you and your husband.

The children and their mother certainly affect your marriage, but at the end of the day, the relationship you have with your husband is the marriage.

When Dannette, vice president of a health provider, married her husband, she moved into the house where he had lived with his ex and their two sons. Because the divorce was amicable, Dannette's husband and his ex remained good friends and, in fact, lived together as roommates up until six weeks before the divorce was final, which made setting up boundaries difficult. "She would just come in to the house to do a load of laundry," Dannette recalls. "One time, she came over to pick up the kids but decided to take a nap first." Dannette's husband couldn't understand why she had a problem with this.

Karen Karbo, author of *Generation Ex: Tales from the Second Wives' Club,* calls it "divarriage" when a couple is divorced but act as if they're still married. If you're in this situation, boundary setting is a crucial step for the health and longevity of your own marriage.

Dannette reports that the ex's behavior changed when they redecorated the house. "We redid every room so it was our home. It sent a signal to her. I remember we were redoing the kitchen. It had been dark, and we repainted it white. When she came into the house, she didn't just run up the stairs and grab something out of the fridge."

Stacy set boundaries with her husband's help. This divorce was amicable, so the ex found it perfectly reasonable to be nosy about private topics between Stacy and her new husband. After several instances in which Stacy's husband responded to personal questions with "I'm sorry, but I feel un-comfortable talking about that with you" or "That's not your business," the ex stopped asking.

Judy remembers having to set boundaries with her husband's ex that reflected her personal comfort levels. "She really wanted to be a good friend, and I didn't see a place for that. Because I'm more of a private person and tend to have very close, intimate friendships, it was very difficult for me to be pursued by her. I had to tell her that just wasn't going to work for me."

There are many ways to handle your relationship with the ex. Your husband once loved that woman enough to marry her and have children with her. She has redeeming qualities. She's a human being just like you, who has fears and insecurities and jealousies that both of you can rise above if you choose to—or, at least, you can. Learn how to shrug off the little annoyances. Concentrate on your husband and your new stepfamily. Keep in mind that no matter how much you think that woman is trying to sabotage your marriage, you and your husband are the ones who determine what goes on inside your relationship.

DISCUSSION TOPICS FOR TWO

1. What is our strategy for handling the ex?
2. If we're in a heated tussle with the other household, how can we calm down and try to look at it from another perspective? Can we learn how to negotiate peacefully?

3. What kind of relationship should we have with the ex? Does it make either of us uncomfortable if it's too close? Too hostile?

4. Are there efficiencies we can develop to make the relationship easier? What about automatic checks for child support payments? How about planning the calendar a year at a time? Can technology make relations easier? E-mail? Cell phones? Fax machines?

5. Do we both understand each other's feelings about the ex? How can we make sure that issues with the ex don't convolute our relationship?

6. How can we make this easier on the kids? What should our response be to the kids when their mother comes up in conversation?

CHAPTER 13

Little Monsters

What to Do When You Don't Like His Kids

CAREER GIRL'S PERSONAL ASSISTANT

1. Be professional. How do I practice nonattachment? How do I not take things personally?

2. Discover your big-picture goals. What is your vision of long-term success? What small things can you do every day to walk toward that vision?

3. Observe your surroundings. What are your stepchildren motivated by? What things seem to make them soften up? How can you use what you know of their individual personalities to make a connection with them?

4. **Prepare your defense.** What strategies do you have in place to stay positive? To defend your marriage against negativity?

5. **Seek guidance.** There's no need to go this alone. Many thousands of families across the country are going through similar terrain. Why not enlist professional help?

Stepmotherhood is more difficult for women who feel pressure to like or love their husband's children. I have interviewed many stepmothers who, with tears in their eyes, have whispered to me that they don't even like their stepkids. Some say they hate them. The words are heavily laced with guilt and shame. Stepmoms don't understand how they can love a niece or nephew without reservation and hate this step-creature they feel they should love.

Sandy never wanted to be a parent. When she married her husband, she acquired two new stepsons who lived in another state. For the entire first year of her marriage she hardly saw her stepsons, but then they started coming to live with Sandy and their father, Tim, every summer. "Every time my stepsons came, I did not look forward to it. I hated it. My husband and I had no alone time when his sons were there. No sex. No nothing."

Sandy admits she was deeply resentful that Tim even had children, though she never let her stepsons see her negative emotions. "I wanted to say to my husband, 'What were you thinking?' I was so pissed no one consulted me about this! You totally screwed up our lives by having these children."

While Sandy was struggling with her feelings about her stepsons, she learned she could not express them out loud to anyone who wasn't a stepmom. "I have a lot of single girlfriends who have kids. If I told them my horrifying feelings, they would say, 'You're out of your mind.' That would make me feel worse. I learned how to talk in front of moms, because they just don't get it. But I needed to hear I wasn't evil. It's really important for other people to say your feelings are okay. Just don't let the kids know you hate them."

Many fathers express openly their desire for their new wives to instantly love their children so they can all be one big happy family. The result is a woman who is trapped by the family she is so valiantly trying to create. Consider how this response from one dad made his new wife feel: "How could you hate a kid?" Wham! It's easy to hate a kid if you feel threatened, or gagged and bound, or taken advantage of, or harassed. As a stepmom, you don't have the same feelings for that kid as his parents do. You don't have the same connection, and yet when kids are challenging, you're still expected to feel unconditional love.

Though you and your spouse should have discussions so he understands you can't feel the same way he does about his kids, be careful about what you share with your husband. Telling your man that you dislike or hate his kids will hurt him deeply and make him feel protective of his kids. Why not tell your best friends your feelings? Then those negative emotions won't be yet another hurdle for your marriage.

Kids Are Not the Enemy

When your household is in crisis, it's easy to make someone into the villain. The kid who is acting out is a popular choice, but it's important to keep in mind that the children have had no control over what has happened to them. They have to play out the drama other people have forced upon them. And just like you, they never asked for any of it. But unlike you, they didn't have a choice.

Everything clicked for Lynn when she realized the children were taking the brunt of all of the adults' actions. And though at times their behavior drove her nuts, she could understand it and because she didn't take it personally, she was able to offer the children compassion. "I was very career-focused and independent and self-oriented. And one big thing I realized when my husband and I got together was that the kids didn't have any say in the situation. They were living out the consequences of someone else's decision, just like I am dealing with these consequences. The kids are not the enemy. They really needed support and stability. They needed to know I wasn't going anywhere."

Considering how adults hurt children when they argue in front of each other, or use the kids as messengers, or bad-mouth the other parent, is it any surprise that a kid will do everything in her power to disrupt the household? If your stepchildren are disruptive above and beyond the normal behaviors of an adolescent or teen, take a step back and consider:

- Are they hearing slander about one household from the other?
- Have they been asked to choose sides?
- Do they feel neglected by a biological parent?
- Are they threatened by your presence because they feel they might lose their father again? (They've already lost him once in the divorce.)
- Have boundaries and rules been lax for the child because the biological parents feel guilty or are so wrapped up in their own problems that they forget to parent their children? If so, the bad behavior could be a call for attention. Children need boundaries and routine to feel safe.
- Are any of the adults in your system relying on the children for emotional support? Are you or any of the adults sharing too much information with the kids about the divorce or your relationships? Children should not be confidants for adults.
- Are the kids being abused verbally or physically?
- Do the children feel any responsibility for the divorce?

Any time you're feeling like a victim in your own home because your stepchildren are acting out or disrupting your life or hurting your feelings, practice compassion. Work hard to see what life must be like for those kids. See if you have the opportunity to teach the children something.

When I'm feeling sorry for myself, I sometimes think negative thoughts, such as "Well, I didn't choose to run out and have kids. I wasn't the one who decided to get married so young and have children. So why do I have to deal with somebody else's decision? It's not fair!" And where do those thoughts lead? Nowhere. I knew what I was getting myself into when I married my husband. I was perfectly aware of his situation. And so, what to *do*? What actions can I take to stop being a martyr? I get to continue making choices every single day about how I will behave.

Sometimes children are given too much power by adults who are unhealthy or freaked out or not paying attention, and that can be dangerous for everyone involved. In these cases, stepmoms feel powerless because the children are able to manipulate the entire household with their behavior. And though the biological parents are the ones who need to step up and parent those kids, sometimes a parent doesn't do what needs to be done. They let the kids run wild and treat a stepparent with contempt. That's where your job becomes extraordinarily difficult. And your work has to be so consistent. So subtle.

Darcy dealt with new stepmotherhood by using the skills she'd perfected as a human resources manager with her two stepchildren. "First, you can't treat everyone the same. You have to find out what motivates each person and use that as a means to an end. Then you let them know your expectations so they can successfully meet them. If they do meet them, I reward them. If they don't, then I help them find ways to be successful. People want to meet your expectations. But if expectations are not set well or clearly, that's when you have a problem. It works with direct reports and with kids."

The more time you spend with your stepkids, the easier it

will get for you to have an influence on them because you'll be more familiar with what makes them tick. So at the beginning, have patience with the kids as much as possible. And have patience with yourself, too. You're all in a new situation, one none of you has been in before. It takes time for everyone to figure out their place in the new system.

Early on in our relationship, before we'd all moved in together, I told Arne I would watch the kids for him at my place while he went Christmas shopping. It was the first time I was left alone with them and I had it all planned out. We would make Christmas cookies by hand, the way I used to do with my grandmother when I was kid. I had a mix that I'd received at a Christmas party, and all we had to do was add butter, flour, milk, and eggs to the mix. The kids were excited; they stuck their hands in the mix, and so did I, letting it squish and squelch between our fingers.

While the cookies were in the oven, we made Christmas cards for their dad. So far, all was going well and I was quite pleased with myself. I'd never been much of a babysitter, and in the corporate world I had few opportunities to be around kids. So I thought the relative calm was a major accomplishment. Then the oven buzzer went off, we each ate two cookies, and I could almost see the sugar blasting into their bloodstreams. What had been a workable volume of chatter went to eardrum-shattering chaos. For about ten minutes they ran around like little yipping dogs after a triple dose of espresso.

All I could do was watch in horror as they zipped from one couch to another, up and over the living room table, around and around the foyer, into my bedroom, then into and out of the bathroom. They played drums on the furniture and screamed at one another and slammed doors. A part of me remembered enjoying similar frenzies in my own childhood. A bigger part of me could only stand paralyzed. Finally, I turned on a movie and sat them all on the couch. Then one got hurt wrestling with another. Pretty soon, two were crying and one was yelling.

I sat in the middle of the room trying to adjust the VCR, feeling suddenly filled with hostility at these kids. They made me feel totally helpless, and they were violating my personal sanctuary with such cacophony that all I could think about was getting them out of my house. When Arne called me from the road to tell me he was on his way, I told him he had better get there as quickly as possible to pick up his children.

The kids were at this point crying for their daddy, and I was mad at their daddy. Yet when Arne walked in the door, they started crying because they didn't want to leave me. Make up your minds! I thought. And then I beat myself up thinking thoughts like "They're just kids," "They have been through a confusing time," "Have an open heart, Jacque! Don't be so selfish! You're a horrible person!"

Arne took them out the door, and the moment they left, I sat down on my couch. That night I refused to answer the phone. I watched a movie, hung out, ate dinner on my own while I just listened to the silence of my once-again-peaceful apartment. I thought about leaving Arne for peace, for quiet, for the life I lived before I met him—take-out on the couch and old movies and the blissful, unemotional, even-keeled silence of a well-ordered, no-surprises kind of life.

But the next time I saw the kids, everyone was calm. They were charming little angels who petted me and hugged me and asked for my attention. I thought, "Maybe I can handle this after all! This isn't so bad! I can do it!" The more time I spent with them, the more I figured out where I could fit in. I began to feel more empowered to be an adult who could maintain the boundaries of behavior expected in our household once we all moved in together.

Tension 24-7

There's nothing worse than living in a household under siege, where screaming, fighting, and crying are the most common forms of communication and high levels of stress are just part of your existence. During times when everyone is vying for power and their place in the family, it's hard to feel any hope. In this kind of situation, when kids are out of control with anger and resentment, it's absolutely crucial to have some powerful coping mechanisms in place.

It's hard to remember anything at all in a heated moment besides the fact that you're angry or hurt or offended. It's nearly impossible to think clearly enough in the middle of a big conflict to recall that your stepchild is a wounded soul, when you want to slap him silly for mouthing off to you after he's skipped school again. That's why it's so useful to not allow the conflict to escalate to the point where you don't have control over your emotions. For most stepmoms in high-conflict households, it's better to avoid big confrontations. Sometimes all you can do is just be there for your husband as he deals with his difficult child.

"If you've got older teenage kids and there's extreme conflict, the only role a stepparent should have is to support their spouse," says counselor Bonnie Rudden. "Let the biological parents take care of it if the kids are really acting out. The parents have to come up with a plan for that child, if possible. The kid doesn't want the stepparent to be there in it. The most you can do is be there for your spouse. As a stepparent, you don't have to feel like you need to fix it. If you get involved, you're going to get blamed."

Stephanie knows what it's like to get blamed by a rebellious teenager. "It never got better with my stepson. Sometimes I thought I would die—there were so many horrible things. I counted the days until he would leave for college. And you're not supposed to take things personally, but it's still hurtful. I knew I was never going to have children and so this was the only child I would ever have. I was so disappointed. I'm sure he saw me as controlling and screwed up because he'd had no boundaries. All he'd had was total indulgence." When this out-of-control kid moved in with Stephanie, a professor, and her husband, Luke, for six of his most tumultuous years, Luke asked her to be an active parenting partner. She was thrown into the role of having to discipline a stepson who threatened suicide, was nearly arrested, used drugs, and regularly broke curfew.

Stephanie is sad to know that even if her stepson suddenly had a change of heart today and called to apologize, she wouldn't believe him. And yet she can see why her stepson acted out, even though she's still so pained about their relationship. "You've got to feel bad for him in a way. He wanted the discipline to come from his parents, not his stepmom."

Allison found ways to cope by carefully developing her compassion and by taking responsibility for her own behavior when her teenage stepkids were jerks. "Sometimes when I would see them asleep in their beds, I would think it's like they're in a field hospital. And they all need nurturing and compassion. I kept having to tell myself, 'I'm the adult. I'm the adult.' And when I felt like my head was turned all the way around in its socket, I would take myself for a walk. I figured one day the ice would start to melt. And every time I felt rejected by the kids and my husband wouldn't step in, I'd have to think about what I really wanted in my life. I had always wanted to be married and have a family. And every family goes through periods of distance and coming together. I could become childlike or I could grow up. Being a stepmom is like boot camp in a way. And you can either become better or be bitter." Allison decided to become better.

Sometimes there is absolutely nothing you can do but smile, nod, and go get in the bathtub. A stepmother has to walk a fine line of remaining involved and staying at a bit of a distance. That is hard to do when someone is hurting your feelings on purpose on a regular basis or even trying to break up your marriage. If those children hate you and do everything in their power to make your life hell, you've got to know how to keep their actions separate from your own self-worth. If you're dealing with a really nasty kid, make doubly sure you've got a solid support network of family, friends, and qualified professionals. Above all, don't give up hope. It was a long time before I could make peace with my parents and stepparents. In fact, I was well into my twenties. But kids grow up. And every day we can learn more about ourselves to make the journey less bumpy for ourselves and for our stepfamilies.

DISCUSSION TOPICS FOR TWO

1. Write down the good qualities and behaviors we see in our troubled stepchild/child.
2. What kind of help does our troubled stepchild/child need?
3. What can we do to behave consistently toward the kids?
4. How can we support each other so we feel strong enough to deal with a troubled child? Can we approach this as a problem-solving team instead of letting a child put us at odds?
5. How can we work on our marriage in the middle of a crisis?
6. Can we both accept that the other person might feel differently about the children in the house? Can we understand that and empathize with our partner?
7. What are our greatest strengths as a couple? How can we use them to sustain our energy and optimism?

CHAPTER 14

* *

He Says

Fathers Speak Out About Their Needs

CAREER GIRL'S PERSONAL ASSISTANT

1. Gauge needs. What does your husband want?
2. Build a partnership. How can you and your husband effectively run your stepfamily? What parenting strengths do you both have and how do you complement each other?
3. Edit yourself. Are there things you say to your husband that are hurtful to him?
4. Maintain your connection. Can you empathize with your husband's feelings? What can you do to support your bond?

5. Perform quarterly reviews. Check in with your husband regularly to assess your family. How are you feeling about your family right now?

Let's not forget about the reason we're all in stepfamilies: men! What do you think it's like for your husband to be in this part-wonderful, part-painful arrangement? As the connector for every member in a new stepfamily, many a man feels caught in the middle of the relationships between his children and new wife, and new wife and ex-wife. It's impossible to give all the competitors for his attention exactly what they want, so dads often end up feeling as if there is no way to win.

When Jake's two daughters fight with Debra, his wife of less than a year, he feels at a loss. "To me, it's 'Oh my God, how do I fix this? Things were great five seconds ago, and now we have conflict.' So what can I do to get everybody back to happy as soon as possible? I don't know what to do sometimes, and I just want to go out in the garage and sit. I don't do that, but that's my initial reaction."

As the new wife to a man with kids, try to keep in mind what's going on inside your man even while you're in the middle of a huge transition yourself. Joshua Coleman, author of *The Lazy Husband: How to Get Men to Do More Parenting and Housework* and *The Marriage Makeover: Finding Happiness in Imperfect Harmony,* is a psychologist with an adult daughter from his previous marriage and twin sons from his current marriage.

"Husbands are really in a loyalty conflict," he says. "They often feel guilty toward their children about the divorce and sad about whatever disruption there has been in terms of their decreased time with their children. Often, they're much more worried about their children than their spouses know. On the other hand, they want their wives to feel happy and cared about and don't know how to divide their time and attention.

"Part of my goal is to help dads talk about how trapped and caught in the middle they feel. Since the average man is not that great at laying out his feelings, it often builds up until it comes out as blanket blame or criticism of his new girlfriend or wife. He may have very unrealistic ideas about how quickly the children will want to bond with her and get angry that she's not making it all better."

So as you head through the tumultuous years of finding where you fit into a family that existed before you came along, remember that this is challenging for everyone involved, not just for you.

Caught in the Middle

Many dads talk about what it feels like to be stuck in the middle. As you've most likely figured out by now, you're not the only one who needs your man.

Erik is the father of four children, ages 7 to 16; his new wife, Julie, has been a part of the family for two years. He describes the feeling. "It's like being a referee. 'Dad, we want to do this.' And then, 'Honey, I want to do this.' You know you're going to disappoint somebody, so who's it going to be this time?"

Coleman explains that it's easy for people in a stepfamily to feel that they're losing out when their needs aren't being met, but the anger or hurt that causes ends up resting on Dad's shoulders. "The biological parent often feels like they're in a no-win situation because they are caught between trying to balance the resources when there are not enough. Those resources are time and money. You know there is often a lot of love to give, but if you don't have the time to give to that person, they are going to start feeling resentful. So I think the biological parent feels very much caught in the middle."

Especially during the early years when everyone is still trying to figure out where they stand and the kids are reeling from the divorce, you can get some high-conflict situations that can derail a brand-new marriage if not handled with care.

"The hardest part for me is figuring out how I support my wife while she is adjusting to her new role of going from no family to having a husband and two stepchildren, but at the same time making sure that my kids know I still love them and I'm still as much on their side as I've always been," says Jake of his new family. "I don't know who has the toughest role in all of this. Sometimes I think the kids do; they have all this junk to deal with because their parents couldn't get along. Sometimes I think my wife has it the hardest. Sometimes I think I do. It's an ongoing internal struggle for me."

Todd felt as if he worked really hard juggling his new family when he married journalist Diane and brought his two sons into the marriage. "I was always nervous about keeping everybody happy," he says. "I have these two kids and they have needs and desires. I have this wonderful new wife and she has needs and desires. And I am in the middle."

Mark only sees his daughter, who lives out of state, a few times a year. He believes that he earned his difficult place in the middle, so he stuffs all of his own feelings in order to make peace. "It's my fault. I'm the one that brought them both into the deal," he says. "I should deal with my pain and not voice my opinion. How my wife feels matters. How my daughter feels matters." See what I mean, ladies? They're hurting, too.

It's About Time

After a dad goes through divorce, the amount of time he gets to see his children typically decreases quite dramatically. Imagine for a moment how you would feel if you had your own children whom you saw every day. Now, suddenly, you can't see them any time you want. Suddenly you have to go for a week or more without seeing them, and every time you do see them, they've changed. They look older. They've had experiences you know nothing about. On top of that, they might be mad at you about the divorce, so when you are together you don't connect very well.

It's a tough transition for Dad to make. The hours he does have with his children are precious to him. "I have four children from my first marriage and I only get them every other weekend," says Erik. "I have less than forty-eight hours twice a month to spend with my kids and I try to spend as much of that time with them as I can. My wife says she feels kicked to the side or that sometimes she feels like she's not even there, even when I try to include her in everything. She says she wants to be involved, but then she says she needs time away. Having only four days with the kids, I want to spend as much quality time with them as I can. Just because I'm divorced and have a new wife doesn't mean I have to stop being a dad."

We have to remember that our husbands were fathers before we came along. It hurts them to think they are being bad fathers. They want to be there for their children. And as new wives to men with kids, we cannot stand in the way of the relationship our men have with their children. A child without a father is at risk.

"In the past two decades there has been an awakening related to the contribution that men have in children's development," says Ken Canfield, founder and former president of the National Center for Fathering in Kansas City, Missouri. "The research is very clear that children who have an involved father who is loving, supporting, and helping them, do far better in school, are less susceptible to peer pressure, less likely to have a child before they're an adult, and have a greater ability to make decisions. Giving access to a father can in almost every case be an asset to that child."

So what can we do to help our husbands stay connected?

"One of the most positive things a stepmother can do is take moments to talk to the father of the children about her relationship with *her* father," Canfield says. "It forces the stepmother to do a couple of things: First, assess a father's contribution to his children and reflect in a way that will help the father understand how powerful and important his role is.

"The second thing is to plan and make sure there is adequate time and the support to make that investment. If a father fails to be responsible with that relationship with the child, in the long term it will impact his current marriage. Encourage a father even though there may be feelings of remorse, guilt, shame, perhaps because he caused the breakup of the first marriage. Encourage him to go forward for the sake of his sons and daughters. Help him look beyond his own issues so he can reach out to his children."

As you're going through this transition from single woman to stepmother, consider what your husband has lost. It will help you better understand him and will ultimately strengthen your marriage.

Communication

It's vitally important that you and your husband learn to communicate and get your emotions out on the table. A stepfamily in the beginning is a fragile thing, and you want to do everything you can to strengthen those bonds. As I've said all along, you've got to have a solid relationship with your spouse. Learning how to talk to each other creates a healthy foundation that you can use to approach all of the stressors in your lives from a position of power.

In a stepfamily, when you work on communicating your needs and desires to each other, remember to think about how what you're asking for will affect your husband. Think about what he must give up to respond to your request.

"When you ask your husband to make a sacrifice so he'll feel like he's not being a good dad, try to have that at the back of your mind," Coleman says. "I stress that, because women often mistake men's more stoic presentation around their feelings for a greater degree of resolution than they feel. But most men in stepfamilies feel a certain degree of torment about it or guilt or worry or anxiety. If you are negotiating with your partner around that, you want to be able to speak to that. You want to lead by empathizing."

So if your husband sees his kids only a few nights every week or month and you've got a big work event that coincides with a visit from the children, ask yourself if you really need him there with you. Consider what you're asking him to give up.

"I feel badly for the man. You love your children. You love your new wife, and they both need to know you're there for them. What an impossible situation. I have a lot of empathy for the men in that situation," says author Anne O'Connor. "I try to remember that when I want to tell my husband something. It's hard to remember when you're really not getting what you want or need. When you're angry, sit down once a week with women and talk about it and vent your feelings. You can never expect a husband to listen to you vent about his kids. You can't rant. You can speak respectfully, but you can't rant about someone's kids, no matter how much right you think you have."

Your husband absolutely loves his children, and he's going to feel defensive if you bad-mouth his kids—even if he agrees with you. So be gentle and respectful of his feelings if you need to bring up a gripe about one of the children.

What He Wants

What do our husbands want? Well, first, they want you to understand their position.

"I want my wife, Debra, to understand how my children are feeling and to understand that as their father I can get mad at them and two seconds later I've forgotten about it and that's just part of being a dad," Jake says. "She doesn't feel the same way about them. She cares for them and has feelings for them, but it's different. She gets upset with them and holds onto it."

Second, they want you to be able to relax and roll with it a little better. I know at the beginning it was easy for me to get tangled up in the smallest things, such as a kid putting the dishes in the dishwasher facing the wrong direction. Finally I had to ask myself, "What's the big deal? Who cares if a kid puts the dishes into the dishwasher facing a different direction than I do?" I mean, come on, the dishes are in the washer instead of left somewhere to rot and stink. This is a good thing!

The fact is, life in a stepfamily is full of compromises, and how well you do can be determined by how you and your husband negotiate and how well you can let things roll off your back. "Sometimes you just have to let things go," Jake says. "In a perfect world we'd do a lot of things differently, but you have to let it go or it will drive us crazy and eat us alive."

Chris has two sons and a new baby with his wife, Dannette. He also advises stepmoms to be flexible. "When you come in as the new female in this relationship with your ideas of how you want things to work, don't get so committed to your way. Figure out what are the important battles to fight and where you can be flexible about how the existing family does things. You have to recognize that their habits have been around a while and it's tough to change."

Dads want their wives to participate and engage with their children. "If the stepparent doesn't get involved with the kids, if you're around but not doing anything to help with the kids, that ruins the relationship between the two adults," Brad says. "You have to jump in and give it one hundred percent no matter whether you're the biological parent or the stepparent."

When you disengage and lock yourself in your bedroom or refuse to go to the park or insist on hanging out with your friends every time the kids are over, the children will ask where you are and why you don't want to spend time with them. They'll take it personally.

Realistic Expectations

Just as we stepmoms have to root out the expectations we bring to the marriage that might be causing hurt or conflict, dads, too, bring their own ideas to the family of how they want things to go. But everyone needs to acknowledge that in a stepfamily the rules are different. Dad has to accept that as the new wife and stepmother, you start as a stranger to those kids. And therefore he must accept how stepfamilies differ from first families.

"In a nonblended family, if people are making sacrifices for the children, they can feel like, 'It's for our children. It's reasonable that we make sacrifices,'" Coleman says. "But in a situation where there is not a biological tie, the stepparent often feels like, 'Well, they ain't my kids. It's noble that *you* want to make sacrifices for them, but *I* don't necessarily want to.' Nobody likes saying or admitting that because it sounds so cold and selfish, but that's the reality. The more that parents and stepparents can feel comfortable trying to have everyone's needs factored in, the better off everyone will be."

Brad told Gretchen right upfront that his priority was to be an involved father to his children. "The first time I met my wife, I told her that my kids come first, and if you can't accept that, then there's no reason you and I should be dating because my children will always come first. I had to be upfront. We might have something planned, but if one of the kids gets sick, sorry, I have to stay home."

Since Brad voiced his needs right away, he and Gretchen were able to discuss the things they found important for family life. They both made the commitment to dedicate time to the children to make them feel wanted and loved, and to provide a welcoming home for them. "We focused more on the kids because I only had them a couple of days a week plus every other weekend. When we were with them, we never got a babysitter. Fifty percent of the time we could do our thing. That made a huge difference. It made a big impression on the kids and solidified their relationship with their stepmother. They felt confident that she was going to be around."

Perhaps the most important realistic expectation to have about your new family is this: It's going to take a while for a feeling of normalcy to develop.

"It's a grind sometimes and you don't want to live in that, but this takes time," Jake says. "There are good weeks and bad weeks. I want to enjoy the good weeks when everybody is getting along, fix the things that need to be fixed, and not dwell on the negative."

Seeing the Big Picture

Dads have their own vision of how they want their families to turn out. And that vision helps them get through the day-to-day, just as it can help us. Many dads voice their desire for their families to feel normal and comfortable instead of the foreign, walking-on-eggshells mess they so often are at the beginning and at so many points along the way. "I want our family to feel normal," Jake says. "I want everybody to respect each other and care for each other and understand where everyone else is coming from. I want us to enjoy each other's company without a constant cloud hanging over the four of us. I hope that cloud shows up less and less often."

Mark and his wife have been together for eight years, and though it hurts him to know that his wife will never feel as close to his daughter as he does, he can understand it. Still, he hopes that in time they will have a solid relationship. "I want it to feel normal and not forced. If twenty years down the road I'm not here anymore, I would hope that my wife and my daughter would still have a relationship."

Erik's vision of the future is pretty realistic. "There are so many things that will make it successful. I don't think it's about having everybody like each other, or love each other, or have this idea that we'll be a cohesive unit as if we were a 'regular' family. I think you're successful if, first and foremost, your marriage is strong and the bio parent and the stepparent are able to work everything out. You can't lose sight of the marriage because of issues with the kids. Another measure of success is if the children knew their father was always there for them and their stepmother cared about them and was a positive influence in their life."

Now that he and his wife have been together a decade, Todd hopes his two teenage sons look to his wife, Diane, as a resource when they are out on their own. "I hope they see my wife as somebody they can come to and ask advice from. And that they feel they can get emotional or intellectual support from her. I think they value her more than she realizes."

And isn't that the crux of it all? How can we realize, in the moment, that we are changing these people's lives? When do the kids like us enough? Can you give yourself credit for the relationships you are creating? Can you feel confident in them? Even though it may take decades to see it, your step-children are affected by everything you say and do.

When my stepchildren suddenly start using a turn of phrase that I use, I get a little feeling of satisfaction. Even though they don't know it right now, I am affecting their worldview. I am having an influence on their lives and their perceptions of themselves. By walking beside them for a while on their path through life, I am modeling a way of life they haven't seen until now. And that's a valuable contribution.

When I treat their father with respect and love, they see that, too, and it makes a difference. Your husband is the reason you're in this new stepfamily. You've made a choice to be with him, faults and all, just as he's chosen you. And when those kids all finally move out of the house for good, what kind of relationship do you want to have with him?

DISCUSSION TOPICS FOR TWO

1. What is Dad's role in our stepfamily?
2. How does it make Dad feel when there is conflict between Stepmom and the kids?
3. What can Stepmom do to help Dad?
4. Have we learned communication skills that will help us negotiate the challenges of stepfamily life? Should we take a marriage education class? See a counselor?
5. Do we both feel heard and understood by each other?

CHAPTER 15

Baby on Board?

What Happens When You Add a New Kid to the Mix

1. **Use problem-solving skills.** How will you solve parenting differences with your spouse? What is your strategy for dealing with jealousy from your stepchildren?

2. **Build community.** How will you make your family feel like a cohesive unit? What traditions will your family celebrate?

3. **Express your opinions.** Now that you're a parent, too, you have more say in what happens in the lives of your children. Many stepmothers find they have to

renegotiate roles with their partners. How will you express your opinions while maintaining a strong bond with your husband?

4. **Develop a time line.** How will you continue to develop your relationship with your stepchildren? When will you do things with them one-on-one now that the baby is here?

5. **Report your findings.** Do whatever you can to get alone time with your partner so you can give each other feedback about how things are going now that the new baby has arrived. When can you get away?

Once upon a time you dreamed about having kids of your own. Then you met and married the man of your dreams, but he already had four children. What do you do? Do you still want a baby of your own? What if your husband doesn't want one? What if you try but can't have one because you've waited too long? Should you adopt? How will a new baby affect the fragile peace you've achieved with your stepfamily? Will a child pull everyone together or tear you all apart? Will you be able to treat the kids equally? Is it okay to love your biological children more than your stepchildren? What's fair?

The decision to have children is complicated enough for couples in which no one has any offspring from previous unions. But throw in a couple of stepkids, a vasectomy, and a woman in her forties, and you've got the makings of a serious family drama.

Do I Want a Baby?

Remember back to when you were a cool single gal and you went to visit your friends with kids to get a "baby fix"? I know when I played with my friends' babies it was always fun, but I was glad to go home and leave the kids behind with their parents. Stepmotherhood is an extended stay with other people's kids. And you get more than your fix. In fact, it's very common for stepmothers to reconsider whether or not they want children of their own after living with stepchildren.

"It was hard because my stepchildren were five and nine when we met and I had never been around smaller children like that. It made me think that I wasn't sure I wanted kids of my own. It was such a shock. Your personal space is so violated," says Darcy, who did end up having two children with her husband. "People always said, 'You knew what you were getting into,' but I didn't. How could I?"

Since the addition of a new member of your stepfamily unit will spark a transition for everyone involved (the ex, too), it's important to consider everyone's feelings. If you think having a baby is going to make your stepfamily feel like a real family, you may be in for a surprise. Consider your reasons for having a baby. Make sure you and your husband are doing it because you want a child.

An infant can help mend rifts between stepfamily members, since there is someone who now shares blood with everyone in the family. However, a new baby can also divide a stepfamily because, in some cases, the involvement of the father with his new child makes his older children feel left out.

Spend some time thinking about your desire for a baby. Consider what your life will be like if you don't have one. How will you feel? Will you feel resentful? Sad? Have you always wanted to have your own kid? Now consider the other side. What do you think your life will look like if you add another member to your family?

Welcoming a New Baby

If you do get pregnant, it's a time to celebrate and to prepare. You pick out which room in the house the baby will sleep in. You choose furniture and start collecting pacifiers and cuddly little blankets. But there's more to do when you welcome a baby into a stepfamily.

First, you and Dad have to tell the kids you're pregnant. Then your husband has to reassure his kids that he won't love his new baby more than he loves them. And you will have to make an effort to do things with your stepchildren so they don't feel left out. These are the same things that parents in first families have to do with a firstborn child when a new baby comes along. You might have to deal with some flare-ups with the kids, but your child won't be an only child. Yours will have older siblings to play with or look up to. Which is wonderful, and can help a stepmother feel more connected to the family.

"Having my daughter made me understand there is no 'them or me.' When you have your own child you really deeply understand, right to the core, that love is not a zero-sum game where because you love your child you can't love someone else," says my stepmother, Nancy, of having my little sister. "When it comes to your marriage and your children, there is enough love to go around. I like that my daughter has grown up with siblings. And I am old enough to see a day when I won't be here and she really has a sister and brothers. Her children will have cousins."

But a new baby can also create upheaval in your couple relationship. Up until now, you've remained a bit on the outside as the stepparent. You've let your husband take the lead in parenting his kids and have bitten your tongue more than once. But now, you have a baby that is part you and part him. You don't have to keep your mouth shut anymore if you see this child—or your husband—do something you don't approve of. It's critical that you and your husband communicate openly about how you're going to parent your new child and how this will affect your role as a stepparent. Many stepmothers find they are much more relaxed about issues they used to get worked up about once they have a child and can understand the feelings a biological parent feels.

Have a summit meeting with your spouse before the baby is born and work through how you want your baby raised in your stepfamily household. You'll have to discuss your parenting styles all over again.

If you're a career woman who has decided to stay home with a new baby, think about ways you can avoid feeling bored, trapped, or stuck. You used to have a lot more freedom when the children in the house were your husband's kids.

It's common for new mothers to ignore dads after a baby is born, so make sure you and your husband continue to do things together. Go on dates and have a babysitter come over to watch your child so you and your husband can continue to feel like a team. You still have to present a unified front to all of the children in the house.

Helping the Other Kids Adjust

Be forewarned that a new baby can be difficult for stepchildren who have already experienced the loss of time with their father. They could already be supersensitive to anything that feels like "Dad is creating a new family because he wants to get rid of the old one."

"If a baby comes along, many kids feel like they're being replaced," says clinical social worker Patti Kelley Criswell. "That's a time to really honor the stepchild. Tell them they can give you something no one else can."

Counselor Bonnie Rudden agrees and advises new parents to really be clear with their stepchildren about how this baby will add to their lives and not subtract from them. "How the kids will do when you have a new baby all depends on how the parents handle it. A new baby changes dynamics in any family. In a stepfamily, the kids have already experienced loss; then you add another baby in there and the kids wonder, 'Am I going to lose my dad because he's going to love this baby more than me?' That's a common thing for kids to go through, so the parents have to say, 'I have enough love for you, for this baby, for everybody in our family.' Kids need to be secure in that area."

Take note. It doesn't matter what age the children are when you add a new baby to the family. They will still need to work through the emotions it evokes, such as fear, jealousy, and sadness. Even adult children have a hard time adjusting.

The good news is that most of the time a new baby, who is just an innocent little bundle of love, can serve as a bridge between the members of a stepfamily.

Darcy has two stepchildren, and when she and her husband decided to have two more, they didn't know how the older kids would take it. "We told the kids I was pregnant after the first trimester and they were really excited initially. My older stepdaughter was upset for a while because she didn't know what would happen. I think there was a lot of fear that Dad would spend all his time with the new baby. But when we had my son, it was awesome. The kids were at the hospital. Number two came along shortly thereafter and the kids were just as excited. They had been asking if we were going to have another one."

Kids' fears about losing time with a parent when a baby is born are not without foundation. Susan D. Stewart, a researcher at the University of Iowa, published a study entitled "How the Birth of a Child Affects Involvement with Stepchildren" in the May 2005 issue of *Journal of Marriage and Family*. Stewart found that a new baby can reduce the amount of involvement the parents and stepparents have in the lives of their children from previous marriages, so having an "ours" baby does not always act as the bonding agent adults hope for.

Brooke grew up with a stepmom who did not have any kids of her own when she met and married Brooke's father; the couple later had a son and a daughter. "Because it was my stepmother's first family, my father has put so much emphasis on making that family work. I feel like I'm not a part of it," Brooke says. "Not that he's pushed me out, but it's like a little exclusive family. My part in that family has fallen by the wayside because he's tried so hard to make it perfect for my stepmother. I'm just this other daughter. He's a great dad. He just stopped being so involved in my life. His sole focus was on the little kids."

Brooke watched her father become a different man from who he was when she was a child. It hurt her to see him become an active father—even though she loves her little brother and sister—because he didn't do the same for her when she was little.

A new baby can at the same time bond a family and bring up challenging feelings for the children. I was 16 when my sister was born and it was thrilling. I held her and played with her. It was cool to have another girl in the family since I had grown up with two brothers. And I love my sister. I don't call her my half-sister. She's just my sister. She's my family.

Still, there are moments when I feel a little twinge of envy that she's had such a different life from mine. Her parents never got divorced. My dad, stepmom, and sister form a mini-family within our larger stepfamily that is separate. When we're all together for a family vacation and the three of them walk off together in front of the rest of us, it hurts my heart just a little bit, even now, to know that I never had that kind of family. That my first family fell apart. Even though I feel included and loved by them, I am still outside.

So, stepmoms, remember: Kids need their dads. Foster that relationship. Help make it strong, and everyone in the stepfamily will be better for it. You're not the only one who feels like an outsider. Even if you never have an "ours" baby, you and your stepchildren's father have formed a new family that excludes the kids to some degree, no matter how nice you are to them or how much they love you. Go easy on them. Try to understand what it must be like from their point of view. I don't know how my stepchildren will react if their dad and I decide to have a child together, but I do know they feel both happy and sad that I'm in their lives at all. A few years ago my stepson and I were talking and he said, "If I could build anything, do you know what it would be?"

"What?" I asked, intrigued because he is always coming up with creative new inventions.

"A time machine so I could go back in time to when my mom and dad met and fix things."

He paused and I kept quiet.

"But then, I wouldn't have met you," he said.

And we talked about how you can be happy and sad about the very same thing at the same time. No matter how much we get along, or how hard I work to make them feel included in our stepfamily, there will always be a little pain for them mixed with the joy. I get it. I don't like it, but I get it.

Feeling Different

You will feel different about your own children than you do about your stepchildren. How could you not? As much as you come to love your stepchildren, they are still someone else's kids. When you have a baby of your own, you'll feel different, and that's just the way it is. So why whip yourself into a frenzy of guilt? Why not just accept that fact and then do the best job you can to foster a connection between your child and her half-siblings, and make things feel as fair as you can to the kids?

Lauren is a doctor who has three stepsons and later had three sons with her husband. "When I had my own children I was able to really see the difference between unconditional love and the more conditional love we stepmoms struggle with. When you're a parent of your own kids, there's an infinitely larger supply of love and forgiveness. I had a more finite supply of those things with my stepchildren. I say this without a lot of pride. I don't think I was a successful stepmother at all."

Part of the reason she doesn't think she was successful is that she treated her own kids different from her stepsons. "I developed a very clear understanding that my feelings for my own biological children were intensely different from my feelings for my stepsons. Those became some pivotal conversations between my husband and me. I had difficulty with some of my stepsons' behavior and acting out. And when they went off to college, I wasn't willing to have those young men come home for the summer. We found other places for them to stay." Her own children have been allowed to stay home during summer breaks from college. Though it's clearly unfair, the kids rose above their stepmothers' actions. "I expected the older boys to have some resentment about that, but the younger boys and the older boys are intensely protective of each other."

Eleanor has two stepsons and an "ours" son with her husband. "We have always raised them as brothers," she says. The older two boys are 16 and 21 and the youngest son is 7. "There is no sibling rivalry. They protect each other. There's such an age difference, there's no competition. Even now that the oldest is in college, he'll make sure he can make it to his little brother's birthday party." Eleanor's son thinks the world of his older brothers. "He thinks they hung the moon. He's in first grade and he's got a brother who drives and another in college. My stepsons have been so loving with him since the beginning. If anything, I'm the one who's hard on my son, because he's mine. But he enhanced our family. He made it even more whole."

Will a new baby make your stepfamily better? It depends. How well can you communicate with your husband and stepchildren? How fair can you be? Can you get out of the way and let your stepchildren develop relationships with your children? Just like all of the other issues stepfamilies have to deal with, the more flexible and creative you can be, the more your stepfamily will thrive.

He's Had a Vasectomy

Every year more than 500,000 men have a vasectomy. (That means he's had surgery so there's no sperm in his ejaculate.) This does tend to complicate things if you want to have a baby together. A vasectomy reversal surgery is clearly not as easy as foregoing a condom or discontinuing the pill. Because the number of remarriages has increased so dramatically in this country, the number of vasectomy reversals continues to climb. The reversal costs anywhere between $5,000 and $15,000, depending on the doctor and how complicated the surgery is going to be. It is typically not covered by health insurance.

The success rate of impregnation after a reversal decreases depending on the length of time since he had the original surgery. If he had his vasectomy less than three years ago, you have approximately a 76 percent chance of getting pregnant. If he had the surgery between three and eight years ago, the chances drop to 53 percent; between nine and fourteen years, you've got about a 44 percent chance of getting pregnant. If it's been more than fifteen years, your chances drop to 20 percent. So if your man has had a vasectomy, make sure you both talk early on about whether or not you want a child together, because the sooner he gets the reversal, the better are your chances of having a baby.

When You Can't Have One

If you met your husband after you've already made the decision not to have a baby, don't be surprised if you still feel grief or resentment about it later on. Before Mary met Pat and his five children, she was divorced from another man with whom she did not have any kids. "I never really had the burning desire to have children, like some people. When I got divorced I was about 30 and I had already decided it was better to not be married and not have kids than be married and unhappy."

Yet the decision still haunted her. She dated her current husband for eleven years before they married. "There was a point in our relationship where I had a little bit of resentment and anger about not having my own baby. At first when we were still dating, my husband said, 'Yeah, we could have kids.' Then later he said, 'What am I thinking? No, I can't have another child. It's too much.' I resented him for that."

Gretchen had a similar reaction. Early on she had decided that if she wasn't married and pregnant by age 35, she wasn't going to have a baby. "I went through a natural grieving process knowing that I was probably not going to have biological children," she says. "But I had made a decision that I didn't want to be a kindergarten mom at age 50."

When she joined her new stepfamily, Gretchen's husband, Brad, asked her to be an active parenting partner to his two children and she stepped up to the plate. "My mother had twelve children and she said, 'I've never seen you driven to have kids, but just because you didn't give birth to the children doesn't mean you're not a good parent. You earn that. It's what you do, not what you say, that kids pay attention to.' I've never forgotten that."

But what happens if you don't make the decision? What if your husband doesn't want to have any more children? Or worse, what if he says he does at the beginning, but then changes his mind after the wedding? If that's your case, get some help dealing with the anger and grief you're bound to feel.

Cheryl's partner David is fourteen years her senior. When they met, he already had four children from his first marriage. He had absolutely no desire to have any more and told Cheryl that upfront. "Deciding not to have a baby of my own was intellectually easier than coming to terms with it emotionally. That was the hardest part for me. I had to mourn that I wasn't going to have a child of my own. I had to express that loss." To help ease her feelings of grief, Cheryl negotiated with David. She told him she wanted him to be an active grandfather so she could be an involved grandma. He agreed. In that way, Cheryl has been able to have children around her that she considers her family.

Judy married her husband a month before her thirty-fifth birthday. "I didn't think I could have a career and new children and bring that much stress into my new relationships. I was concerned how a baby would impact the children. I will never completely know if not having a baby was the best choice for me. But I do believe it was the best for the family."

Some women are unable to conceive. Sarah and her husband tried for years to have a baby, but to Sarah's eternal disappointment, she was unable to get pregnant. It was the same for Cosette. She and her husband went to fertility doctors for help, with no result. Eventually, after years of going through the monthly cycle of hope, expectation, and devastation, they ended up adopting a baby together.

Catherine and James began trying to get pregnant when Catherine was 39 years old. "I told my husband I wanted to try it naturally. If we gave it a year or two and nothing happened, I'd be able to let it go," Catherine says. "So we just stopped using birth control. We kept trying but nothing happened. In retrospect I probably should have investigated all the options to increase my chances. I really did want to have a child. There are still pangs because that seems like the ultimate biological experience. I will never have the same connection with my stepson as I would have with my own child. On the other hand, I'm adopted, and I know it's perfectly possible to have a close and loving relationship with nonblood parents."

If you can't have your own baby, make sure you allow yourself to grieve. It may be a wound you'll have for your lifetime. Still, creating a warm and supportive stepfamily can help you feel fulfilled.

DISCUSSION TOPICS FOR TWO

1. Do we want a baby? Why or why not?
2. How do we think a new baby will affect our relationship as a couple?

3. Will our stepchildren/children welcome a new half-sibling? What can we do to facilitate good feelings?

4. Do we think Stepmom will feel different about the new baby than she feels about the stepchildren? Is that okay?

5. Will Stepmom's child have to follow the same rules as Dad's kids?

6. How will we both feel if we can't have, or decide not to have, a baby?

7. Will you resent your stepchildren if you can't or don't have a baby?

8. Do we make a good parenting team? If not, how can we become one?

CHAPTER 16

Let the Sun Shine

What You Expect Is What You Get

CAREER GIRL'S PERSONAL ASSISTANT

1. Set your action plan. Close your eyes and imagine a peaceful household where everyone in your stepfamily lives in harmony. Ask yourself: What actions can I take right now to move toward that goal?

2. Make a list. Write down ten things you can do with members of your stepfamily to promote community. When will you accomplish the first item on your list?

3. Pay attention to your voice. What are you saying to yourself when you're mad or hurt? How do you describe your stepfamily to other people?

4. **Do what it takes.** What are you willing to do to make your stepfamily work?
5. **Be a key decision maker.** Your mood affects the entire household. Can you decide to be above all the daily annoyances? Can you choose to have a positive, hopeful outlook?

A growing number of studies from institutions, including Yale, the University of Pennsylvania, and the Mayo Clinic, suggest happy people live longer. Attitude really does make a difference, and in a stepfamily it can make all the difference.

David Cooperrider and Suresh Srivastva, at Case Western Reserve University's Weatherhead School of Management, developed a strategy in 1987 to help organizations and corporations improve. The theory calls for companies to abandon a problem-solving approach to organizational development and instead use a strategy called "appreciative inquiry." The basic assumption behind the problem-solving approach is that "an organization is a problem to be solved." Alternatively, the appreciative inquiry approach begins with the assumption that "an organization is a mystery to be embraced."

Cooperrider maintains that problem-solving language assumes and highlights human deficiency, while appreciative inquiry techniques use positive language to focus on dreams and possibilities. He and his colleagues have developed a way to interview members of an organization so that even in the largest corporations, every member has a voice and a vision to help improve the whole, while addressing difficult issues.

You get buy-in from everyone in the company because all involved feel they have an influence.

The techniques employed in appreciative inquiry have since been used in other settings, including marriage and family therapy, as a way to help family members identify and achieve their dreams. In the therapy world, the correlating movement is called strength-based therapy. Instead of working through all the things you hate about your life and trying to come up with ways to solve those issues, you focus on the strengths and build on them. For instance, if you hate the fact that your husband undercuts you in front of his kids when you try to tell them what to do, and you focus on how that enrages you, you're sunk because you're coming from a place of anger and in that space, there is no room for change. You will come at him from an attack mode, and he'll shut down before you even begin to have a conversation.

If, on the other hand, you think first about the ways he does support you, it will create space in your heart to be able to dream of ways you can both find peace. Start with the thought that you and he are partners, and you'll be able to have more productive discussions that end with a positive action. Maybe he insists that the children always say please and thank you when they ask you for something. Or maybe he tells them not to interrupt you when you're talking.

I'll give you an example. When I am angry, I get tunnel vision. My husband usually cooks, but one evening I thought I would make dinner since he'd worked in our yard all day. For two hours I worked to create a homemade meal my mother, a wonderful cook, would have been proud of. We all sat down, and immediately my stepdaughters began complaining about how much they hated the meal. When one stepkid said, "I don't like this," my first reaction was to petulantly think, "Oh yeah? Well, I don't like you!"

Luckily, since I'm an adult, I was able to keep my mouth shut, but I still let their comments affect my mood. It was a Sunday night at the end of a long couple of weeks together, and I was tired. (At least, that's my excuse.) But then my inability to manage my thoughts made everything spiral out of control. Here's how it went down. First, the kids complained, which, as every parent and stepparent knows, they all do. Second, I got mad. Third, my husband became supersensitive to my mood and got angry at the kids. Fourth, the kids picked up on the bad vibes and acted out even more, which put us back where we started, because I got mad again. You get the picture.

What if I had asked myself in positive language what I hoped to be able to achieve with my stepfamily when my feelings get ruffled? What if I had considered my big-picture dreams and goals, so they influenced how I responded to my stepchildren? Here's how the scenario could have been reversed to maintain the harmony that is important to me. First, the kids complain. Second, I realize it is not a personal attack because all kids complain about food. Third, I do something positive. I laugh and say, "Too bad for you guys, good for the rest of us who like it. We get more!" Fourth, my husband laughs. Fifth, I ask all the kids to name their favorite meals and ask who wants to help prepare their favorite tomorrow. Sixth, we finish dinner, do the dishes, and happily go about the rest of our night.

That sounds like a lot more fun. Next time, that's going to be my action plan.

Things You Can Do Right Now

It can be awfully hard to think of positive things if you're mired in anger, self-pity, fear, or any of the emotions on the negative side of the spectrum. So I'll give you a few examples to get you started.

- Do loving things for yourself. Get a massage. Have lunch with your best friend. Go for a walk. Take a yoga class. Check out the new exhibit at your local museum. Listen to beautiful music.
- Interview your stepfamily about the things you all love to do, and then do one of them. Play a board game. Go swimming. Take a bike ride. Go to the movies and get candy and popcorn. Head to the great outdoors and go camping. Cook something together. Visit a greenhouse. Spend the afternoon having a picnic at the park. Visit people you all love. Browse a bookstore. Play catch. Paint. Make a family project, maybe a tree house.
- Practice banishing your negative thoughts and language and focusing on what you desire for your stepfamily. For instance, when I was annoyed and hurt that the kids didn't like the meal I cooked, instead of giving in to the negative thoughts, I could have decided in the moment not to think them. I could have decided that

I was instead going to be happy I get to eat leftovers tomorrow. (Which I am happy about—wahoo!)

- Approach your stepfamily members with love, compassion, or kindness when they are negative to you. For instance, if a kid slams the door on the way into the house, indicating that he's angry about something, then sasses you when you remind him to pick up all the stuff he dumped in the middle of the living room and take it to his bedroom, you've got a couple of options. You could scream at him about how you're an adult and he has to listen to you. (This won't work.) You could ignore him and withdraw to your bedroom where he can't get you. (This will work temporarily but won't foster connection between you and your stepson.) Or you could say something like this: "You seem to be having a rough day. Do you want to tell me about it?" If yes, then you can sit down and talk together and you can gently remind him to pick up his things once he's calmed down. If no, then you can say, "Well, I hope you feel better. In the meantime, could you please take your stuff upstairs?" If he sasses, you respond again with kindness: "I'm sorry you're not feeling well, but we still have to follow the house rules. Please pick up your stuff and take it to your room. Then I'd love to know if there's anything I can do to help." (If you intend to enforce that the common areas are clutter-free, then this will have to be on the list of house rules your husband presents to the kids.) Keep responding with kindness and you will defuse the situation.

- Meditate. Pray. Chant. Visualize. Whatever your spiritual practice is, do it. Meditate every morning about the stepfamily you wish to create. Pray with gratitude for all the wonderful lessons these people are teaching you. Choose to view these people as conduits for your personal growth. Choose to see them as conduits to your faith.

- Decide to have a positive impact. Depending on your actions in every moment, you can either have a positive or negative effect on the people around you. So take responsibility. You decide. You choose. You act.

Have High Expectations

In most stepfamily research and literature, the need for realistic expectations is touted as a crucial ingredient for the successful stepfamily. I agree. It's easier to get through the difficult times if you know that the stage your family is going through is normal.

That doesn't mean you shouldn't have high expectations for your stepfamily. Just because you have an idea of what to expect in the normal development of a stepfamily, such as dealing with loss and grief, guilt, and loyalty issues, that doesn't mean that you should expect your home life always to be challenging. If you choose to expect your stepfamily to develop strong bonds to one another, then do what promotes that expectation, and eventually you will develop those bonds.

It's the old adage: What you expect is what you get. It

might not be right away, but eventually you will create your own reality. You can change people by changing your reactions to them. You change the dynamic of your family with your presence every day without thinking about it. So imagine how powerful you can be if you consciously choose how you want to change it.

When I first decided that someday I would own a company and be my own boss, it was terrifying. I had no idea how to do it. I remember sitting at my desk at home staring off into space and thinking that I was on one side of the Great Wall of China and all the business owners were on the other side. I had no clue how to climb over that wall. So I started small. I made one phone call to another writer who had started her own company and asked her to tell me about how she did it. I took notes. Then I called another one. I talked to a journalist, a novelist, and a business owner who'd started from scratch and asked them how they did it.

My dad gave me an invaluable tool that has served me well all my life, and now I'll pass it along to you. It's his Rule of 20. When I was a kid, he told me that if I wanted to do something and didn't know how, I should find twenty people who are in some way related to what I want to do and ask them about it. He assured me that by the twentieth person, I would know what to do. I've done it over and over again. It works. You have proof of it in your hands: This book started with my question, "How do I become a stepmother?" and grew out of my application of the Rule of 20.

I also use another trick I learned taking acting classes as a young adult. When actors create a character onstage, they go through a laborious process of first reading the play, and then creating a backstory for their character so they know why the character does what she does. We had to practice writing backstories in my class. Then we were told to pick three physical things to do that would express the essence of the character. So, for instance, if I was playing a teenage girl I might chew bubble gum, twirl my hair, and say "Whatever" in a bored voice.

After the class was over, I wondered if I could use the same technique to trick myself into believing I was a self-confident, successful business owner. I imagined what a person like that might do. I was a shy kid, and in my head there was a big gap between how I saw myself and the person I thought I needed to become to start my own business. Because I fidgeted with my hands a lot when I was a shy adolescent, I decided to hold my hands clasped in front of me to keep them from shaking. I practiced looking people in the eye and smiling at them. And finally, I worked on standing straight with my shoulders back.

I practiced and practiced and practiced. And eventually, the more I did it, the easier it got. After a while, my confident physical actions showed up as real self-confidence; people treated me differently because I stood straight, didn't fidget, looked them in the eye, and smiled.

The point of this story is not that you should become an actor or smile and nod all the time when your stepkids are driving you nuts. I'm simply suggesting you can create change if you decide to change—even if at first it feels like pretending. If you focus on something every single day, it will become your reality.

If you want to be a calm, supportive, loving stepmother, what physical things do you think that kind of person would do? Would that stepmother clench her teeth? No! She would self-soothe. She would breathe deeply to relax. She might even pat her own hand through a tough moment to remind herself to have compassion.

Consider a stepdaughter in crisis. Her father, your husband, is out of town and she's home alone with you. She comes home after curfew. You ask her where she was. She yells at you that it's none of your business. She might swear at you. She might even strike out at you. In this imaginary scene, you don't have Dad as backup, and neither does she. So how can you become the stepmother you want to be in that moment? How can you de-escalate the situation?

First, do everything in your power to remain calm. Take a deep, slow breath. If you can't be calm, then quietly tell your stepdaughter that you're glad she's home safe. Then tell her you'll talk to her about it in the morning when you're both well rested. And go to bed.

If you come at her with a calm demeanor instead of blowing your cool, you'll find that you can affect the atmosphere in your house. Do it over and over again. It's true, you may never see any kind of acknowledgment from your stepdaughter, but you know you're acting with integrity and helping another wounded human being who is seeking what we are all seeking: love, belonging, safety, and control over her own life.

You should have high expectations of your stepfamily. No, it will never be a first family, that's true, but it can be a supportive group of individuals who enjoy spending time together and who root for one another. You can develop rituals you do together that make you all feel that you're part of something — that you're all a part of the "in" crowd. You can help foster mental, physical, and spiritual health in your stepchildren as they are launched into the mystery of their adult lives.

And finally, in order to maintain your dedication to becoming the kind of stepmother you want to be, surround yourself with and read about people whom you admire. If you embodied all of the qualities you desire, who would your peer group be? Would they be the stepmoms who are so lost in the quagmire of "woe is me" that they can't see anything but bad behaviors and bratty kids? Or would they be stepmoms who choose to look at those same children and see bravery and amazing skills of adaptation and survival?

Stepmotherhood and motherhood can be thankless jobs, the fruits of which may be invisible for years. You need to cultivate the ability to let things roll off your back and to thank *yourself* for a job well done. I'm about to finish another successful full-time summer with the kids. This Saturday they go back to their mom's house for the school year. We'll still see them three weekends of every month and every Thursday night, but during the summer we have them full-time. We've had a fun summer—though not one without temper tantrums and pouts, fights and screaming matches between siblings. We've had bike outings and swimming lessons. We've gone on vacation together and buried one another in the sand. We've talked about the mysterious meaning of the universe. We've talked about how to find out what you want to do when you grow up. We've had bonfires and roasted marshmallows.

All in all, it's been a great summer. We've all become even closer than we were when it started. And now that it's drawing to a close, I've scheduled a two-hour massage with my favorite massage therapist on the Saturday after they leave because I did a helluva job. I had a meltdown or two but rebounded after time alone and a good sleep. I've snapped at a kid and then forgiven myself. I've allowed them to see who I am. I have spent a few beautiful weekends with my husband. And I have taken good care of myself. Next summer is going to be like this one. Challenging. Fun. A learning experience. An opportunity for grace.

Now, what about you? What do you do well? How do you comfort yourself? Can you forgive yourself for past mistakes you've made with your stepkids, move on, and do something you feel proud of today?

And if you have trouble giving yourself compliments, I'll do it for you. Excellent job, sister! Keep it up. You are a stepmother. You deserve recognition, kindness, and respect from your family. You are capable. You are mature. You're doing a great job and I, for one, am proud of you.

DISCUSSION TOPICS FOR TWO (OR MORE)

1. What do we each want our stepfamily to feel like in twenty-five years? Do we want to feel close and connected to one another? Do we want to see one another

often? Do we want to celebrate one another's victories together?

2. What are our favorite times from our lives together so far?

3. How can we increase the joy and harmony in our household?

4. List all of the attributes we each admire about everyone else in our family.

5. When have you felt the most included and appreciated? What can you do to feel that way every day?

CHAPTER 17

The Payoff

Keep Your Eye on the Big Picture

So what does a woman get out of marrying a man with children? Many women don't see the rewards of stepmotherhood until late in life—if at all.

The idea for this book had many wellsprings, one of which was an interview I conducted for a magazine article I was writing. I was chatting with a surgeon who ran her own practice. She had also been a stepmother of three for more than two decades. All the kids were grown, and she and her husband enjoyed each other's company immensely. She told me she was known by all of her friends and colleagues as a success story. Her stepfamily looked like an episode of the Brady Bunch; it was all happy and smiles and goodwill.

I asked her a few more questions about her stepfamily's dynamics—for instance, how she'd developed a good relationship with her three stepchildren, two boys and a girl, who were all teens when she moved in with them. I asked if her husband was a strong and present father who supported her. I asked about the relationship with his ex. Nothing seemed to upset her. When I asked a more direct question about her relationship with her stepdaughter, I hit a nerve, and this woman spewed forth a stream of venomous rage about her stepfamily life that she'd stored up for years. The resentment and anger and hurt just poured out of her like lava.

I've never written about her, and I've changed identifying characteristics in this telling of the story because this woman didn't want anyone to know her secret: that even though she appeared to be a happy stepmom, underneath it all she still seethed with anger.

I spent several days after the interview thinking about this woman. She felt all the anger and fear and jealousy we all feel, but she'd stuffed it down instead of dealing with it directly and letting it go. It reminded me of the advice my dad had given me just after his divorce from my mother: "You don't have to love your parents, you don't even have to like them, but you must make peace with them. You can't be 65 and still let your parents control your life because you're pissed about what they did to you when you were 5." I thought this advice, slightly retooled, could have been just as applicable to this woman's situation as a stepmother.

You get to choose what the payoff is going to be for you. It starts with what your priorities are. What do you want in the long term? Do you want a strong friendship with your husband? Do you want to have your stepchildren come to you for advice and camaraderie? If you and your husband have children together, do you want all of the kids to love and protect one another? What do you want?

You can build something beautiful with your stepfamily over the long term. Studies indicate stepfamilies that make it have a huge positive impact on the children and adults. Children learn about flexibility and how to get along with different kinds of people. Adults are reportedly more satisfied with their second marriages if they do the work it takes and learn from the past. But you've got to get through those tough years, as you do in any union. We have the power to see our lives exactly the way we want to see them, even if from the outside it looks as if we've got it pretty bad. You get to choose. The thoughts you think every day are what give you power to either sink yourself into depression or uplift yourself by making you feel that you have purpose and meaning.

So pay attention. When you write in your journal about your stepfamily, what are you writing? Is it mostly negative? How do you talk about them to other people? Do you slam them regularly or talk about their good qualities? Can you work to put more positive things in your journal or your thoughts every day? Can you have compassion for the other people in your stepfamily? Can you walk a mile in their shoes?

Right now the reason you're in a stepfamily is because you fell in love with that man you married. In the first years of marriage to a man with kids, when life is like a three-ring circus and the marriage is at its most fragile, it's hard to see what the benefits are, especially after what you've given up to be in the marriage. And your commitment is immediately tested, even though you're still in the process of building a foundation of friendship and lasting love with your partner.

So how do you find happiness and joy when you feel as if you're constantly battling just to keep from bursting into tears? I interviewed stepmoms who have been in their marriages from two years to more than twenty, to see if they had some advice about what they got out of marriage to a man with kids.

I Did It All for Love

Love. That great elixir. It moves people to do things they can't imagine themselves doing—such as marrying a man with a handful of kids who are bruised and battered from divorce or death. It's what we're all here for in our marriages. The love stories we've all heard since we were kids are something to aspire to, but the tales usually end with a first kiss or wedding and totally leave out what it takes to protect and maintain love.

"For a long time I used to beat myself up," says Beth. "What the hell did I do? I used to date young lawyers, guys with nice cars and money. One guy I dated on and off just got married, and he doesn't have any kids. I think I like challenges, because I got one. I believe every marriage is tough. We do have a strong relationship now, but we had to go through hell and back to get here. And now, to see how happy my stepdaughter is, it was worth it."

Lisa's struggle to find her place in her stepfamily is over, but sometimes it's still difficult for her. When I asked her what the long-term payoff for her is, she said, "The payoff is two-fold: One, I now have strong relationships that have sustained the test of fire. Two, I am a much better person because I hung in there and didn't run away."

Tracy and Andrew have developed a strong partnership, and the kids have only added to their relationship. "The ultimate goal is to share my life with a wonderful man. And I look at his kids as being a benefit on top of that. You can learn a lot from kids if you're open to it. There are always good things about kids."

Even though times have been tough for Georgianne since she married T. J., she knows she was meant to be with him. "My husband's an amazing guy. At 43, I had never been married. I am a pretty strong-willed individual and finding a guy who wasn't threatened by that was really hard to do. He is my soul mate. I knew when I met him. I had one of those cosmic flash-card moments, which is not to say we don't have issues. But we're so much on the same page about so many things."

My dad and stepmom often talk about how strong their partnership is now that they've spent a few decades working together to form a solid marriage. "In the normal course, marriages are fragile," Nancy says. "In the normal course, if you have biological children, there's a risk. It's greater when you have stepchildren. There's a time in a marriage when you are tested, and after that you know it's going to last. It's usually after you've had some trouble. That's when the awareness of being separate evaporates and your family becomes just part of who you are."

Arne is a good husband. He is the reason I am able to be in yet another stepfamily. He makes it possible for me to be a stepmother who has developed strong bonds with my stepchildren. At the very beginning, Arne showed the kids how it was acceptable to treat me. He was open to my talking about how it felt to be a stranger entering into his family. He was willing to hash out the details of a new stepfamily. We answered all the questions I posed to you and your husband in this book. And perhaps more than anything, he made me feel important. Without a doubt, he loves his kids with every part of himself, but he doesn't ever make me feel left out of decisions. That way I never feel that the kids come before me or I come before the kids. I am his partner. We are the adults and we both make decisions that affect our family together. And I love Arne with all of his imperfections and his past. His presence in my life has helped me clarify my values.

My top five priorities are

1. My spiritual and personal development and contribution to the world
2. My husband
3. Our commitment we made when we said our vows
4. Raising the children to be healthy, contributing, and confident adults
5. My family

So what are your priorities?

Personal Growth

When the days are so dark it's hard to see that you'll ever make it out to some kind of peace and happiness, some stepmothers focus on their own personal growth.

Stephanie dealt with a teenager who acted out in serious and dangerous ways that made life extremely difficult for everyone in the family. Now that he's out of the house, it's the development of Stephanie's spirit she points to as the payoff for her. "I feel good about the one hundred percent I gave the situation," Stephanie says. "I made a commitment. I feel good about the compassion I gave. You have to adjust to so many things, and I didn't break. I just bent. I feel sad, but I feel good about what I did. I don't feel like a success ... but I wouldn't have been able to live with myself if I had quit, if I had backed down."

Indeed, as a stepmother, you have the opportunity to learn all kinds of things you didn't know about yourself. I have learned how generous I can be, how compassionate and loving. I've learned that even when I feel jealous and horrible, if I just wait it out for a day or two, I can calm down and look at life from the other person's point of view and learn something valuable. There's no doubt I've learned the depths of my own ugliness. I can throw tantrums and cause my family heartache if I'm feeling left out or taken advantage of in some way. But I've also learned I want to be supportive and loving and peaceful. I've discovered what my definition of family is. It's people who are connected to me by life and experience and love and pain. I found out I am fiercely loyal to those I consider my family—fairly few of whom actually share blood with me.

Building a Family

Once Allison made it past the difficult years of moving in with teenage stepchildren, she managed to develop strong relationships with all of her stepkids. "My marriage and my life as a stepmother have had the greatest positive impact on me of anything I've ever done in my life. And I've been able to achieve some pretty big things in my world. I had a company that did $2 billion in revenue when I was twenty-eight years old. I was an entrepreneur. I've had a really big life. To stay with my husband and stepchildren is what I am the most proud of," she says.

My stepmother, Nancy, says, "The payoff is in raising contributing adults. The payoff is in holidays and grandchildren and grandparenthood. You can look at what happens to very successful people with huge social circles and business relationships. When all is said and done, it's your family that shows up when you need them. Your family members are in a relationship with you connected by love and blood and history and not by whether you work together or that your children go to the same school."

Cosette and her husband have been married for twenty years and have been through the ups and downs of life together with her three stepchildren. "I can't imagine my life without these three people in it. That would be a horrible thing to me. I wouldn't be able to stand that. The payoff is so huge. It's about people who value you and know you and that you have even more people who enrich your life."

My stepchildren and I are still building our feeling of family together. Recently they've all started telling me they love me, so I know it's okay to express love for them. They come up and take my hand, so I know it's okay to hold hands. They are not my biological children, but someday they will help decide which old folks home I go to. If that isn't family, I don't know what is.

The Kids

Author and stepmother Anne O'Connor thinks about the big picture. "You must remember the long-term perspective, that it will be okay in the end. Everyone will be okay. That's really hard to remember when the kids are being snotty to your face and you want to smack them. But hang on to the core belief that it will be okay, and it can be a self-fulfilling prophecy."

My mother, Jean, is a stepmother of three, who are all adults now, and after twenty years of marriage to my stepfather she believes she has developed rewarding relationships with my stepsisters and stepbrother. All three of them visit often and occasionally send her cards. "They usually felt comfortable talking to me, sometimes even more so than their dad," Jean remembers. "I view myself as really more of a friend. Now they call me 'step-monster,' lovingly."

Jean attributes her strong relationships with her stepkids to her years spent teaching high school children. She describes her approach as careful and casual at the same time.

She enforced the house rules but made sure fun was a big part of family life. "Being a teacher was key. I had dealt with so many kids my whole life that it made it easier. I wanted my stepchildren to enjoy life and not be tense and uptight. They needed to be kids. They needed to have fun," she says.

When Lauren's three stepsons and three biological sons developed strong sibling bonds, she felt that things really gelled in her family. "Things do come around. They do. To have the boys as six brothers adoring each other and taking care of each other and getting so excited to see each other—to see that bond and receive forgiveness from my stepsons for the things I've done. They really desire my input in their lives."

Judy and David have been married for twenty years and she considers her family a success story. "I think that anybody who remains married and embraces the children as family is successful no matter how poorly or how well they did it, if they did their best and they continue to grow and be open to how they can be family to their adult children. Have I failed them somewhere along the way? Sure, but I am confident I have always given them an opportunity to make it better. You've got to have a personal relationship with the kids. You have to try, go out for breakfast, find something you like to do together. Eventually, it will pay off. They will remember you gave them a piece of yourself. You may not always see the fruit of that, but the only thing we really have to give, when you come down to it, is ourselves."

Heidi stays home to care for her four stepchildren. Even though she sometimes has a bad day, her rewards come in the little things, such as a look on a kid's face. "What's in it for me?

Love. I get this wonderful man's love. And some of the kids tell me they love me. They all like hearing how much I love them. Sometimes when I look at the expression on their faces I get goose bumps. The work is constant and those moments are just once in a while, but it makes it all worthwhile."

Catherine is still dreaming about the day her stepson will acknowledge everything she's done for him. "Ten years from now maybe my stepson will realize, 'Wow, she did love me and do things for me.' I have this little fantasy that he'll say, 'Boy, that must have been hard for you, and thanks for hanging in there.'"

Jenna advises stepmoms to be realistic about the payoff. There are things that as Dad's wife you will not be participating in, most likely, but you get to carry with you the sense of a job well done. "I won't get to go with my stepdaughter to pick out her wedding dress. I'm not the bio mom and there's a lot of stuff I'm not going to get to do. But I still get to feel a lot of pride in things I've been influential in. I get the self-pride that comes because I made a difference."

With my family, I also try to keep my eye on the big picture. For me, the payoff will be to develop strong friendships with my stepchildren. I want to give them something of myself and to remain a stable influence they will come to appreciate in time. We're still relatively new to one another, but the kids have already taught me so many things about being human. They've taught me about my own beliefs about how children should be raised. I've learned they are endlessly forgiving of my foibles as long as they understand them. Most of all, I want us to continue to have as much fun together as we do today.

Vision

Every year two of my girlfriends and I meet for a weekend or an entire week for what has become a career-planning summit. We envision what our goals are for the future and what steps we can take to meet them.

When I do goal setting for my career, I do it in yearly increments. First, I plan what I want to accomplish within a year, then two, then five, ten, fifteen, and so on. I close my eyes and visualize what my life will look like when I hit the milestones I set. I see myself in my office. I think about who will be with me, what new awards and photos will be hanging on my walls, what my office will smell like, and what the view is out the window.

In the second part of the exercise, I set tangible steps to get me to where I want to go, things I can go home and accomplish after our weekend together. First, I identify all the areas I need to work on and then break them all down to the smallest possible steps. For instance, "publish a book" is made up of many steps I had to break down into areas such as find an agent, write a book proposal, and send it out. Then I had to break down those categories even further.

The third part of our career summit is a brainstorming session in which we all work to help one another with contacts or ideas for new directions or efficiencies. The results of our annual weekends have been astounding. All three of us have developed our businesses in the directions we have identified in those meetings. We have all hit our yearly goals and continue to take steps toward the big-picture vision of where we want to end up down the road.

A few years ago I started employing the same process with my personal life. It had worked so well for my career, I thought, why not try it? So now I visualize my goals for my family and then think about the things I can do now to make sure I'm headed in the right direction.

If I want to have a good relationship with my stepdaughter in the future, I might break that down into little pieces that would include taking her to a movie, just the two of us, going for a walk with the dog a couple of times a week, or really listening when she talks to me. Remembering who her friends are. Finding out her favorite foods.

It's those small, everyday interactions that build relationships. And if one day we have a bad stepfamily day in which everyone is in a bad mood, oh well. We'll feel better the next day.

So what is your future vision? Close your eyes and imagine yourself later in life. Where will you and your husband live? What will your house look like? Who will live there with you? Will the children come for visits? What will you do when they arrive? How will you act around one another?

At the End of the Day

When you keep your eye on the big picture and always have that final day in the back of your head, it's easier to let the little things slide. Your family members are the ones who show up when you need them. The people in your family attend your funeral.

Who cares if your house isn't as clean as you like it, or if a kid forgets (again) to put away his dishes? If you are on the path to building a relationship, that stuff will all work itself out. You'll find out where you fit in your family and how you want them to fit into your life. You'll discover what's important to you for the long haul. When everything feels as if it's piling up around you, it's easy to lose sight of a larger vision. But that vision is what can sustain you through the rough patches of stepfamily life. That vision, combined with the traditions you build together and the meaning you create with your family, can build a strong bond between people that makes you feel like family even if everyone doesn't see eye to eye.

It's what you do that leaves a mark on people. Lynn remembers a defining moment in her relationship with her stepson. She was a prepared stepmom and had a legal guardianship document signed by both of her stepson's parents. "I got a call from my stepson's school. He was having an asthma attack and they wanted to know if they could take him to the emergency room and if I would meet them there. I got there in twenty minutes, I flew there, and I had this overwhelming feeling of how important he was to me and just how strong that relationship had grown. He remembers that moment to this day. He says, 'They called you and all of sudden you were there.'"

So what kind of mark do you want to leave? What do you want your legacy to be with your stepchildren? What kind of marriage do you want? You can sustain the love and hope with which you entered your stepfamily. Simply decide to, and make it so.

Panel of Experts

Stepmoms Like Us

The following is a list of career women turned stepmothers quoted in *A Career Girl's Guide to Becoming a Stepmom*. This is only a partial list of the brave women who offered advice to new stepmoms for this project; they are representative of many others who also shared their stories in hopes of lending a hand to their fellow stepmoms. These women range in age from their thirties to their sixties and come from many races, faiths, and economic backgrounds. I have changed names and some identifying characteristics to protect the privacy of the participants and their families. My humble gratitude goes to all of the women and men who willingly spoke with me about personal, and sometimes painful, topics.

Allison
Career: Entrepreneur and interfaith minister.

Stepmother of: Two boys, recently married, and a girl, who just graduated from college. The girl was 12 and the boys were 18 when Allison entered their lives.

Marital status: She was married once before but was single for ten years before she met her husband, Charles, who was in the middle of a divorce after twenty-seven years of marriage to his first wife. Allison and her husband met when Allison was in her mid-forties; they married nine months after their first date. They've been married for ten years.

Beth

Career: Former paralegal and current owner of an Internet business. Beth left her career when she had her own children. She now runs her business and helps her husband with his small business.

Stepmother of: One teenaged girl, who was 8 when Beth met her father and is now 16.

Marital status: Beth met Victor when she was 27. She'd never been married and had no children of her own. They married a month before Beth turned 31. Beth is now 35 and her husband is 43. Victor and his ex-wife separated when their daughter was 8 months old. He was divorced for ten years when he met Beth. Now Beth and Victor have two children together.

Catherine

Career: Actress.

Stepmother of: One son who was 7 when she met him and is now 14.

Marital status: Catherine divorced her first husband before they had children. She met James in 1997 when she was 36 and he was 38. They bought a house a block away from James's ex-wife and moved in together in 1998. They married in 2001. Though they tried to have children together, they were unable to.

Cheryl

Career: An inspirational speaker for business executives who owns her own business.

Stepmother of: At age 53, she is the stepmother of four grown children, three boys and one girl. She is also a stepgrandmother and great-stepgrandmother.

Marital status: Though she's not legally married to David, they have been together for eighteen years. Cheryl was married once before but did not have any children.

Cosette

Career: Marriage and family therapist.

Stepmother of: Three children, a girl and two boys, whom she met when they were 17, 19, and 22; they are now 37, 39, and 42.

Marital status: She and Paul have been married for two decades. They are both therapists and run a private practice together. The couple adopted a child after they found out they couldn't have one. Cosette is now a stepgrandmother, but all of her stepkids and stepgrandkids call her by her nickname, Cozi, which is how she makes them all feel.

Dannette

Career: Vice president of a large health care provider.

Stepmother of: Two boys, who were 2 and 4 when they met, and 4 and 6 when Dannette and Chris married.

Marital status: Dannette was 30 when she met Chris, whose divorce from his ex was final the day of their first date. Dannette and Chris now have a 3-year-old daughter together. They've been married for seven years. Chris and his ex had an amicable divorce, and now all of the adults in this stepfamily system are cordial to one another.

Darcy

Career: Human resources manager for a medical products company.

Stepmother of: At 33, she is stepmother to two children, a boy, 13, and a girl, 17. They met when the children were 5 and 9.

Marital status: Darcy first met her husband, Jud, in 1995. They started dating in 1997 and she met his children that year. Darcy and her husband married in May 1999, when Darcy was 26. They have since had two children together, a girl, now 4, and a boy, now 5. Darcy and Jud's ex-wife have become friends. She even named Jud's ex-wife the godmother of her first child with Jud.

Debra

Career: Product manager at a medical device company. She's also a marathon runner.

Stepmother of: Two girls, ages 7 and 9.

Marital status: Debra and her husband, Jake, met at work when Debra was 27. They moved in together a year and a half after they met, and then married in December 2004. Debra and Jake have been extremely proactive about getting educated about stepfamily issues. They started seeing a counselor about a month after their wedding, and Debra has been in a stepmom support group since four months before she got married.

Diane

Career: Journalist and independent radio producer.

Stepmother of: Two boys who were 8 and 10 when Diane met them and are now 18 and 20.

Marital status: She and her husband, Todd, met when Diane was 30 and married two years later. They've been married for eight years and have worked and traveled the globe together. They lived a mile away from Todd's ex-wife, so the children could easily go back and forth.

Eleanor

Career: In the 1980s, Eleanor worked her way up the corporate ladder at a cosmetics company in New York City while she put herself through culinary school to become a chef. After moving to the Midwest she took a job as a credit supervisor at a major retail company.

Stepmother of: Two boys who were 1 and 7 when Eleanor married their dad. The boys are now 15 and 21.

Marital status: Eleanor and Marty met in college, but Marty married his college girlfriend, with whom he had two children. Eleanor and Marty married in 1992 and have a 7-year-old son who wonders why he can't have two mommies like his older brothers.

Georgianne

Career: Independent consultant for a luxury car manufacturer.

Stepmother of: Four children between 8 and 15 years old.

Marital status: Georgianne married T. J. when she was 43 years old. She'd never been married before, and T. J. had been divorced for five years when they met. The children lived with their mother 150 miles away, but two of the younger kids asked to live with their father, so Georgianne became a full-time stepmother of two. They stayed for three years. Recently, they moved back in with their mother, because Georgianne and T. J.'s marriage was suffering.

Gretchen

Career: Vice president of operations for a marketing company with global clients.

Stepmother of: Two children, a girl and boy, who were ages 5 and 8 when they met and who are now 18 and 21.

Marital status: Gretchen and Brad have been married for eleven years. They met thirteen years ago when Gretchen was 32 and Brad was 38. Gretchen is the primary breadwinner in the family. Brad had a nasty divorce from his ex and Gretchen became the communicator between households.

Heidi

Career: Lawyer for a family court where she often represented the best interests of children. Since marrying her husband, she has left her career to raise her stepchildren, though she plans to return to a legal job.

Stepmother of: Four children, two girls and two boys, ages 8, 10, 12, and 14, who were 6, 8, 10, and 12 when Heidi and John married.

Marital status: When Heidi turned 41, her former high school sweetheart John, whom she hadn't heard from in ten years, contacted her to tell her he was divorced. They married a year later in August 2003. Heidi moved across the country, away from her family and friends, to be with John and his children.

Jenna

Career: Financial adviser at a national retailer.

Stepmother of: Four children who were 6, 8, 13, and 15 when they met and are now 11, 13, 18, and 20. The older two children didn't spend as much time at Dad's house as the younger two, so Jenna is closer to the younger kids.

Marital status: Jenna and Carl dated for three years before they married. She was 32 when they met. They've been married for two years.

Judy

Career: Career-licensed counselor and management consultant.

Stepmother of: Three children, a girl who was 2, and two boys who were 6 and 8 when Judy met them. The kids are now 22, 26, and 28.

Marital status: David and Judy met when Judy was 34 years old and the couple married four months later, just before Judy turned 35. Judy had been married once before but was single for ten years when she met David. Now the couple has found a combined purpose by helping other married couples in their community.

Laura

Career: Corporate attorney.

Stepmother of: One girl who was born six months after Laura and Rob met. Rob's daughter is now 3.

Marital status: Laura and her husband, Rob, met when Laura was 24, after her sister introduced them. Rob had never been married before, but a former girlfriend he dated for only two months called to tell him she was pregnant. Rob and Laura met six months before the baby was born. The first year of their marriage involved a paternity suit and visitation battles with Rob's ex-girlfriend. Laura and Rob have now been married for two years. Rob recently won his paternity suit and visitation rights to his daughter.

Lauren

Career: Doctor. Lauren, now 49, retired a few years ago. She plans to redefine herself with an as-of-yet unknown new career in the coming years.

Stepmother of: Three boys who were 4, 7, and 9 when Lauren met their dad, Tom, and 7, 10, and 12 when they married.

Marital status: Lauren met Tom when she 21. They dated for three years before they married. He was the junior vice president of a bank and she was a teller. After they married, Lauren went back to school to become a doctor. Tom had full custody of his children and they had three boys together after they married; two of them are in college and one is in ninth grade. Lauren and Tom have been married for twenty-five years and are still in love.

Lisa

Career: Corporate executive.

Stepmother of: Two, a boy and a girl who were 5 and 7 when Lisa met them. The kids are now 18 and 20.

Marital status: Lisa has lived with her partner, Liz, for twelve years. Lisa often felt isolated and lonely as a woman in a stepmother role with another woman's children. When the children were young, Lisa and Liz had them 65 percent of the time.

Lynn

Career: Former communications expert who went into family services after she became a stepmother, and now owns her own stepfamily coaching business.

Stepmother of: Three children, a boy and girl, who were 10 and 11 when she met them, and an older boy who never lived with them. Her husband, Vincent, had full custody of the younger children.

Marital status: Lynn and her husband, Vincent, have been married for ten years. They have two daughters together, a 6-year-old "ours" baby and a 3-year-old girl they adopted.

Marie

Career: Account manager and media relations director at an advertising agency.

Stepmother of: One stepson, who was 9 when she met him and is now 21.

Marital status: Marie met her husband, Grant, when she was 23. They dated for three years and were engaged for one year before they married. Grant is thirteen years her senior. He had one son of whom he had 50–50 custody when they met. Marie and Grant have two children together. They've been together for twelve years.

Mary

Career: Nurse.

Stepmother of: Five children who were between the ages of 3 and 9 when Mary met them.

Marital status: She and her husband, Pat, dated for eleven years before they married. During that time, Mary kept her own house. Mary and Pat never slept in the same house when the children were around. When Mary and Pat tied the knot, three kids were in high school and still living in the house and the other two were in college. Mary knew all of the children very well.

Monica

Career: Financial planner.

Stepmother of: A grown stepdaughter who was a teen when Monica married her father.

Marital status: Monica and Ben have been together for fifteen years and married for eleven. They met while Ben was in the middle of his divorce from his ex, to whom he'd been married for twenty-five years. This couple chose not to have any children together and have focused on developing a harmonious union. They are very clearly close friends and love each other tremendously.

Nancy

Career: President and CEO of a national nonprofit association.

Stepmother of: Three adults in our thirties, a girl (me!) and my two younger brothers. We met my stepmother when my brothers were 7 and 9 and I was 11.

Marital status: My dad, Ron, and my stepmother, Nancy, have been married since 1985. They have a daughter, my younger sister, who is now 17.

Sally

Career: Singer who makes a living as an executive assistant.

Stepmother of: Four children between the ages of 7 and 16.

Marital status: Sally and Abe have been married for two years. They met through an online dating service and married a year after they met. Sally was married once before to a man with whom she ran a business, but they didn't have any children. She was single for four years before she met Abe.

Sandy

Career: Account manager at a print and Internet media company.

Stepmother of: Two boys, 8 and 10 when Sandy and Tim married, now 17 and 19.

Marital status: Sandy, now 45, and Tim, now 44, met at a football game when Sandy was in her late thirties. They've been married for nine years. Both of Tim's children live in another state with their mother; he sees them during holiday breaks and over the summer. Sandy was married once before and divorced. She was single for six years when she met Tim. Sandy never wanted children, and she and Tim have struggled with her feelings of indifference toward his children.

Stacy

Career: CEO of a publicity agency.

Stepmother of: Two girls who were 7 and 12 when she met them and are now 10 and 15.

Marital status: Stacy has been married to her husband, Travis, for one year. They met taking ballroom dancing lessons. They have since performed in amateur dancing competitions. Stacy is 38 and Travis is 44.

Stephanie

Career: An English professor.

Stepmother of: One boy who was 12 when Stephanie married his father and is now 24.

Marital status: Stephanie and Luke married twelve years ago when she was in her forties. Luke had nearly full custody of his son, whose mother was a "visiting aunt kind of person," according to Stephanie. She and her stepson do not have a good relationship today, and she doesn't think they ever will.

Sue

Career: Manager for an electronics retailer.

Stepmother of: Two children, a boy and a girl, now 19 and 22. The children were 4 and 7 when the couple married.

Marital status: Sue met her husband, Matt, when she was in graduate school earning her M.B.A. They dated for five years before they married, when Sue was 28. They have been married for fifteen years and have a 2-year-old daughter together. Sue and Matt were involved in ongoing legal battles over custody and visitation with Matt's ex-wife.

Tracy

Career: Demographer and social scientist.

Stepmother of: Two boys who are now 16 and 20. They were 12 and 15 when Tracy met their father.

Marital status: Tracy married her husband, Andrew, in 2003. They met through an online dating site in 2001. She was married once before for eight years and was single for six years before she met Andrew. She was in the process of adopting a daughter when she met him; they have raised the child together. A week after she and Andrew married, she turned 40.

Resources for Stepmoms

Websites

Stepmoms

www.comamas.com
Supports stepmoms and moms who want to work together for the sake of the children.

www.secondwivescafe.com
An online forum for second wives and stepmoms to share information and find support.

www.secondwivesclub.com
An online community for second wives, this site has online journals, discussion boards, and links to stepfamily information; includes a list of lawyers, counselors, and mediators.

www.stepsforstepmothers.com
Has a posting board for stepmothers.

Stepfamilies

www.stepfamilies.info
The official site of the National Stepfamily Resource Center at Auburn University in Auburn, Alabama. This organization replaced

the Stepfamily Association of America in 2006 and offers professionals and families educational materials about stepfamily life. Read more about it under organizations.

www.bonusfamilies.com
Provides information, links, and resources for stepfamilies.

www.sharekids.com
An online coparenting tool that helps divorced parents keep track of their children, with a calendar, expense calculator, and emergency information.

www.stepfamilyinfo.org
Includes articles and quizzes for stepfamilies, remarried couples, and coparents.

www.successfulstepfamilies.com
A site with information to support Christian stepfamilies.

Legal Issues

www.nolo.com
Includes legal information and do-it-yourself documents for wills, divorce decrees, and prenuptial agreements.

www.supportguidelines.com
An online resource with information about child support laws in the United States.

Marriage Education

www.divorcebusting.com
Marriage and family therapist Michele Weiner-Davis provides information about how she works with couples all over the country to strengthen their marriages.

www.gottman.com
Marriage expert John Gottman's official website with quizzes for couples and information about Gottman's work, books, videos, and workshops.

www.marriagefriendlytherapists.com
Cofounded by expert marital therapist William J. Doherty, the National Registry of Marriage Friendly Therapists is a resource for couples looking to find a highly qualified therapist. The registry only accepts therapists with advanced experience and training.

www.smartmarriages.com
The official site of the Coalition for Marriage, Family, and Couples Education. The site includes a list of marriage education classes and resources.

Parenting

www.aboutourkids.org
The site of the New York University Child Study Center includes a library of articles on topics such as parenting, growth and development, and school and learning issues.

www.cyfernet.org
The site of the Children, Youth, and Families Education and Research Network offers research-based parenting information about kids of all ages. Includes what to expect during developmental stages.

www.kidshealth.org
Site with a vast array of information on children's health and developmental stages.

Services

www.maids.com
A team of cleaning professionals who take the job off your shoulders.

www.nannynetwork.com
If you're a full-time stepmom and can afford help, the Nanny Network can help you find someone to help you with the kids.

Books

For Stepmothers

The Courage to Be a Stepmom: Finding Your Place Without Losing Yourself by Sue Patton Thoele (Tulsa/San Francisco: Wildcat Canyon Press, 1999).
Sue Patton Thoele is a psychotherapist and stepmother whose book provides lots of sound advice for learning how to be a stepmom.

Encouraging Words for New Stepmothers by Jean McBride (Fort Collins, Colorado: CDR Press, 2001).
In fifty-one essays, this book addresses the emotional issues a woman new to a stepfamily faces. It's a good book to keep on the nightstand for times when a stepmother is feeling jealous of an ex, hurt by a stepkid, or angry at her husband.

The Enlightened Stepmother: Revolutionizing the Role by Perdita Kirkness Norwood and Teri Wingender (New York: HarperCollins, 1999).
Advice from stepmothers of all ages, occupations, and lifestyles about what works and what doesn't when taking on the role of stepmother.

Generation Ex: Tales from the Second Wives Club by Karen Karbo (New York: Bloomsbury, 2001).
Karbo offers statistics, anecdotes, and insights for second wives and stepmoms, served up with wicked humor.

Second Wives: The Pitfalls and Rewards of Marrying Widowers and Divorced Men by Susan Shapiro Barash (Far Hills, New Jersey: New Horizon Press, 2000).

The experiences of second wives are covered in detail, such as revenge tactics inflicted by first wives and dealing with past and present in-laws. Comments from attorneys and counselors are interspersed.

Stepmotherhood: How to Survive Without Feeling Frustrated, Left Out or Wicked by Cherie Burns (New York: Three Rivers Press, 2001).

Cherie Burns is a journalist, mother, stepmother, and stepgrandmother who originally published this book in 1985 and was one of the first people to write about the dark side of stepmotherhood. She addresses all of the negative emotions a woman can feel in a new stepfamily, and her suggestions help by including interviews with stepmoms as well as with the leading researchers in the field of stepfamily dynamics.

Stepwives: 10 Steps to Help Ex-Wives and Stepmothers End the Struggle and Put the Kids First by Lynne Oxhorn Ringwood and Louise Oxhorn, with Marjorie Vego Krausz (New York: Simon & Schuster, 2002).

Helps moms and stepmoms put together a working relationship that benefits both houses, and especially the children.

Effects of Divorce

Between Two Worlds: The Inner Lives of Children of Divorce by Elizabeth Marquardt (New York: Crown, 2005).

After surveying 1,500 adults and interviewing 70 in depth, Marquardt, a child of divorce herself, presents true stories of how divorce changes the lives of children.

For Better or for Worse: Divorce Reconsidered by E. Mavis Hetherington and John Kelly (New York: Norton, 2003).

The initial two-year study of how preschool children and families responded to divorce grew into a thirty-year endeavor tracking long-term effects upon the participants. This comprehensive study of the stages of divorce, remarriage, and the resulting stepfamily relationships shows how choices can lead to a path of healing and fulfillment.

The Unexpected Legacy of Divorce by Judith Wallerstein, Julia Lewis, and Sandra Blakeslee (New York: Hyperion, 2001).
Wallerstein tracked a group of children of divorce for twenty-five years and found lasting effects upon them as adults.

We're Still Family: What Grown Children Have to Say About Their Parents' Divorce by Constance Ahrons (New York: HarperCollins, 2004).
Ahrons debunks the myth that children of divorce are troubled underachievers who lack the ability to form lasting relationships. Children of a landmark study are interviewed twenty years later.

Life in a Stepfamily

Becoming a Stepfamily: Patterns of Development in Remarried Families by Patricia L. Papernow (Cambridge, Massachusetts: Gestalt Institute of Cleveland Press, 1993).
Describes the stepfamily cycle of development and how four kinds of typical stepfamilies travel through the seven stages. Aimed at therapists, it's a good read for anyone in a stepfamily.

How to Win as a Stepfamily by Emily B. Visher and John S. Visher (New York: Brunner-Routledge, 1991).
Written by the founders of the Stepfamily Association of America, this guidebook for remarried families addresses legal and financial issues as well as new family dynamics with former spouses and new grandparents.

The Smart Stepfamily: Seven Steps to a Healthy Family by Ron L. Deal (Minneapolis: Bethany House, 2002).
Presents practical, realistic solutions that honor families of origin while developing new stepfamily traditions. The book is based on Deal's nationwide stepfamily seminars and focuses on ways to build healthy marriages and peaceful families within the Christian faith.

Stepfamilies: Love, Marriage, and Parenting in the First Decade by James Bray and John Kelly (New York: Broadway Books, 1999).
A comprehensive guide to easing the conflicts of stepfamily life, based on Bray's nine-year study of one hundred stepfamilies and one hundred nuclear families. The book focuses on Mom-Stepdad families.

Stepfamilies and the Law by Margaret M. Mahoney (Ann Arbor: The University of Michigan Press, 1994).
A readable account of stepfamily law in the United States.

Strengthening Your Stepfamily by Elizabeth Einstein and Linda Albert (Atascadero, California: Impact, 2005).
Experienced as both stepfamily counselors and stepparents, Einstein and Albert give solutions for stepfamily parenting. Among topics addressed are myths, unrealistic expectations, decision making, effective communication, sound discipline, stepsibling rivalry, and noncustodial parents.

The Truth About Stepfamilies: Real American Stepfamilies Speak Out About What Works and What Doesn't When it Comes to Creating a Family Together by Anne O'Connor (New York: Marlowe, 2003).
Personal experiences from stepfamilies across the country provide the basis for a highly readable book about strategies that work to create a cohesive stepfamily.

Weddings, A Family Affair: The New Etiquette for Second Marriages and Couples with Divorced Parents by Margorie Engel (North Chicago, Illinois: Wilshire, 1998).

This practical guide covers how to plan nontraditional ceremonies and handle thorny etiquette issues faced by couples and their extended families.

Yours, Mine, and Ours: How Families Change When Remarried Parents Have a Child Together by Anne Bernstein (New York: Norton, 1990).

The author's personal experience as a stepmother and a mother of an "ours" child is combined with interviews of more than fifty similarly blended-family households.

For Kids

The Dinosaurs Divorce: A Guide for Changing Families by Laurence Brown and Marc Brown (New York: Little, Brown, 1988).

Cartoon dinosaur characters help children navigate the scary questions that surround divorce, such as "Why did Mom and Dad divorce?" and "What will happen to me?" This book is for children ages 4 to 8.

Divorced but Still My Parents: A Helping Book About Divorce for Children and Parents by Shirley Thomas and Shirley Rankin (Longmont, Colorado: Springboard Publications, 1997).

The five stages of mourning (denial, anger, bargaining, depression, and acceptance) are interspersed with interactive activities in this book for children ages 6 to 12.

Help! A Girl's Guide to Divorce and Stepfamilies by Nancy Holyoke (Middleton, Wisconsin: Pleasant Company Publications, 1999).

A self-help book for girls ages 4 to 8, based on letters from girls to *American Girl* magazine.

It's Not Your Fault, Koko Bear: A Read-Together Book for Parents and Young Children During Divorce by Vicki Lansky (Minnetonka, Minnesota: Book Peddlers, 1998).
This read-together book helps children ages 4 through 7 recognize and talk about feelings when faced with changes brought about by divorce.

Mama and Daddy Bear's Divorce by Cornelia Maude Spelman (Morton Grove, Illinois: Albert Whitman, 2001).
Children in preschool through grade 1 identify with Dinah Bear as she describes her favorite people, activities, and things and how each is affected by her parents' divorce.

Two Homes by Claire Masurel (Cambridge, Massachusetts: Candlewick Press, 2003).
The author creates a sense of security for young Alex, who is confronted with Mommy and Daddy's separate homes.

What in the World Do You Do When Your Parents Divorce? A Survival Guide for Kids by Roberta Beyer and Kent Winchester (Minneapolis: Free Spirit, 2001).
Addresses fears children have when their parents divorce. This book gives children examples of ways to talk to adults about their worries. For children ages 7 to 12.

For Parents

How to Talk So Kids Will Listen and Listen So Kids Will Talk by Adele Faber and Elaine Mazlish (New York: Avon Books, 1999).
First published in 1980, this classic guide for both parents and stepparents can be used to foster communication in the house.

Mom's House, Dad's House: Making Two Homes for Your Child by Isolina Ricci (New York: Fireside, 1997).
A classic, first published in 1982. Ricci addresses legal, emotional, and practical realities of creating two happy and stable homes for children.

Financial Information

For Richer, Not Poorer: The Money Book for Couples by Ruth Hayden (Deerfield, Florida: Health Communications, 1999).
A money class in a book that helps couples learn to view their financial lives as a partnership.

Money Advice for Your Successful Remarriage: Handling Delicate Financial Issues Intelligently and Lovingly by Patricia Shiff Estes (New York: iUniverse, 2001).
A guide to financial systems, options, and solutions that work in remarried households as well as how to deal with the complicated emotions connected with the subject of money.

Organizations

American Association for Marriage and Family Therapy
703–838–9808
www.aamft.org
The website provides a nationwide listing of marriage and family counselors, plus links to marriage education resources.

American Bar Association, Family Law section
312–988–5603
www.abanet.org/family
The website includes a lawyer locator and information about legal topics such as family law and estate planning.

American Coalition for Fathers and Children (ACFC)
800–978–3237
www.acfc.org
The ACFC works on creating family law and legislative and public awareness about what happens to fathers in divorce. The organization promotes the idea that both parents share custody and responsibility of their children in order to better their kids' lives.

Association for Conflict Resolution
202–464–9700
www.acrnet.org
Includes a list of mediators across the country.

Coalition for Marriage, Family and Couples Education (CMFCE)
202–362–3332
www.smartmarriages.com
This group based in Washington, D.C., produces the Smart Marriages conference annually as part of its mission to serve as a connector between mental health professionals, clergy, and lay educators whose goal is to educate couples about marriage.

National Center for Fathering (NCF)
800–593–3237
www.fathers.com
The mission of the NCF, based in Kansas City, Missouri, is to improve the lives of children by helping dads stay involved.

National Council on Family Relations (NCFR)
763–781–9331
www.ncfr.org
Based in Minneapolis, the NCFR serves as a forum for family researchers and educators. The organization develops materials to aid and promote healthy families. It produces two professional journals: *Family Relations* and *The Journal of Marriage and Family*.

National Stepfamily Resource Center at Auburn University (NSRC)
www.stepfamilies.info
stepfamily@auburn.edu
A vast resource for stepfamilies, the National Stepfamily Resource Center develops educational programs for stepfamilies and the professionals who work with them. Dr. Francesca Adler-Baeder, director of the Center for Children, Youth, and Families at Auburn, oversees the NSRC, which serves as a clearinghouse of information

for stepfamilies that links family science research on stepfamilies and best practices in work with couples and children in stepfamilies. The organization's website includes links to resources for stepfamilies, frequently asked questions, and research summaries. The NSRC also publishes *Your Stepfamily* online magazine, which offers articles on stepfamily life.

Stepfamily Association of America
See the National Stepfamily Resource Center above.

Acknowledgments

First of all, this book would not exist if I hadn't attended a book release party for Abigail Garner's publication of *Families Like Mine: Children of Gay Parents Tell It Like It Is* (HarperCollins, 2004). I watched Abigail bravely use her own history to help other people and was brought to tears by her inspiring words. I thought if she could do it, maybe I could, too. My agent, Joy E. Tutela, offers the kind of guidance and attention writers dream about. I am forever grateful for her vision and encouragement.

To Stacey Barney for believing so strongly in this work and helping to shape its form. To Jennifer Pooley who offered insightful comments to sharpen the manuscript. And to Jeanette Perez, whose thoughtful direction brought this book to fruition.

While researching, I interviewed and read the materials of many stepfamily experts and marriage and family therapists whose advice and research influenced my thinking and writing. In particular, I'd like to acknowledge and thank Francesca Adler-Baeder, James Bray, Cherie Burns, Joshua Coleman,

Patti Kelly Criswell, William Doherty, Margorie Engel, P. M. Forni, John Gottman, Ruth Hayden, Jan Hoistad, Karen Karbo, Margaret M. Mahoney, Perdita Kirkness Norwood, Pat Love, Anne O'Connor, Ann Orchard, Patricia L. Papernow, Lynn Roberts, Diane Sollee, and Michele Weiner-Davis.

Barbara Haugen read the manuscript early on and helped me avoid making a fool of myself with my comma problem. Rosanne Bane offered words of wisdom along the way. My parents, Jean, Arnold, Ron, and Nancy, gave me the background I needed to write this book as well as love, patience, and constant support. I also couldn't have written this book without my brothers, John and David, my sister, Kate, and stepsiblings Marilee, Kevin, and Cindy.

My stepchildren are the best stepkids a stepmom could ask for and I feel privileged to be part of their lives. They are such polite, kind kids who embraced me with open arms from the very beginning. Our relationships continue to deepen and become even stronger. I can hardly wait to see which retirement home they choose for me. And to Arne, my husband, who shows me every day that successful, happy, and loving stepfamilies are a reality.